MAKE SUCCESS MEASURABLE!

A Mindbook-Workbook for Setting Goals and Taking Action

DOUGLAS K. SMITH

John Wiley & Sons, Inc.

New York • Chichester • Weinheim • Brisbane • Singapore • Toronto

Library of Congress Cataloging-in-Publication Data:

Smith, Douglas K., 1949-
     Make success measurable! : a mindbook-workbook for setting goals and taking action / Douglas K. Smith.
          p.   cm.
     Includes index.
     ISBN 0-471-29559-0 (cloth : alk. paper)
     1. Goal setting in personnel management.   2. Performance standards.   I. Title.
     HF5549.5.G6S647   1999
     658.3'14—dc21   98-44988
                                                                                CIP

10   9   8   7   6

CONTENTS

INTRODUCTION

This is a how-to book. It explains how you and your colleagues can set the performance goals that matter most to your customers, to your shareholders, and to yourselves. It also lays out the managerial disciplines you need to achieve the goals you set. If you read and use this book, you will learn how to:

- Set goals that are specific, aggressive, and achievable.

- Set goals that matter to customers who want speed, quality, and value at a fair price.

- Set goals that matter to shareholders and funders who want a return on their investment and funding dollars.

- Set goals that matter to you in terms of opportunities, rewards, skills, and membership in an organization with strong values.

- Link the goals that matter to you to the goals that matter to customers to the goals that matter to shareholders and funders.

- Set nonfinancial as well as financial goals and link them together.

- Identify and use familiar and unfamiliar metrics that are relevant to today's most pressing performance challenges.

- Understand and use outcome-based goals that support success, while avoiding activity-based goals that produce failure.

- Set and commit to goals that challenge your minds and your hearts.

- Use the concept of working arenas to get beyond thinking only about "my job."

- Use the concept of working arenas to coordinate and align your goals with the goals of others throughout your organization.

- Understand how the time it takes to achieve different goals can help you see when and whether those goals fit together and make sense.

- Convert new visions, strategies, and directions into achievable outcome-based goals that can galvanize yourself and others in your organization.

- Choose when to use the team discipline to achieve your goals and when to use the working group discipline to achieve your goals.

- Choose when to use the horizontal/process management discipline to achieve your goals and when to use the vertical/functional management discipline to achieve your goals.

- Choose when to use the discipline of behavior-driven change to drive organizational success and when to rely on the decision-driven discipline.

- Build an outcomes management system to drive performance and personal development throughout your organization.

I believe you will benefit from this book because the challenge of setting and achieving performance goals has become very confusing. It has been more than 30 years since Peter Drucker wrote about the importance of managing for results. His work led to the widespread practice of management by objective. But an awful lot has happened in the past 30 years. The world of business and organizations has changed dramatically, turning many of Drucker's specifics (though not his wisdom) upside down. In the aftermath of total quality, customer service, time-based competition, strategic alliances, globalization, reengineering, core competencies, continuous improvement, innovation, teams, horizontal organization, benchmarking, best place to work, information technology, diversity, environmentalism, deregulation and reregulation, eCommerce, and privatization, those of us left standing in today's organizations are unsure about what performance goals and outcomes make the most difference and why. We know that setting performance goals is key to managing ourselves and others, but we no longer know how.

We continue to manage by objective. But the vast majority of our objectives are mere activities, or what I call "activity-based" goals. We set goals and objectives to *pay* better attention to customers and their needs, to *team up* better across the organizational silos, to *build* core competencies, to *reengineer* our processes, to *globalize* our management, and so forth. In doing so, we have utterly confused the distinction between the *outcomes* we are attempting to achieve and the *activities* by which we hope to achieve them. Activities are not and should not be objectives. Activities are *how* we achieve the objectives—the outcome-based goals—we set for ourselves. Activities are essential to our success. But activities are not goals. A major purpose of this book is to familiarize you with the distinction between outcome-based goals and activity-based goals and to help you set and achieve more of the former.

Nor do we routinely differentiate among the most critical management disciplines needed to achieve the performance goals we set. Most of us continue to manage in one way, and one way only. Regardless of the nature of the challenge at hand, if we are bosses, we give direction, delegate responsibilities to individuals, monitor, and follow up. That is, in fact, *one* powerful way to manage. But it is only one of several management disciplines for delivering performance. Today, there are many other disciplines. This book will describe the major disciplines you need to use and help you figure out when you need to use them.

The book is organized in four parts. Chapters 1 through 4 provide the background, concepts, tools, techniques, and frameworks you need to set specific outcome-based goals that matter to successfully navigate today's most pressing performance challenges. Chapters 5 through 7 focus on helping you align and coordinate goals throughout your organization. Chapters 8 through 10 describe the management disciplines you need to achieve your goals and how to make choices among them. Chapter 11 concludes the book with a step-by-step design for building an outcomes management system in your organization.

Here's what you'll learn from each chapter.

Chapter 1 starts with an explanation of the critical distinction between activity-based goals and outcome-based goals. It identifies the problems and misguided assumptions you need to overcome to avoid activity-based goals, including the pitfall of goals that are strictly financial. Chapter 1 reminds you that today's performance challenges demand outcomes that are both financial and nonfinancial, and that those outcomes must simultaneously benefit customers, shareholders, and the people of the enterprise and their partners. It introduces you to the *cycle of sustainable performance,* a logical framework you can apply to ensure that your organization's goals reflect a truly balanced scorecard.

Chapter 2 helps you articulate and pick metrics that make success measurable. It describes the difficulties and challenges in using the unfamiliar metrics so often required by today's new performance requirements, and it introduces you to the *four yardsticks*—four families of metrics you can apply to set goals for any challenge you face.

Chapter 3 reviews the SMART criteria that you must use to articulate outcome-based goals that are specific, measurable, aggressive and achievable, relevant, and time-bound. It encourages you to set *and* achieve goals by following an iterative cycle of performance that includes setting, pursuing, evaluating, achieving, and/or adjusting goals continuously. Finally, Chapter 3 describes how to use a powerful logic device called a *performance tree* to break down any broad challenge you face into the set of specific goals that are most important for you and your colleagues to achieve.

Chapter 4 expands upon the familiar notion of *stretch*. Everyone knows how important it is to aim high. By using stretch goals, we can achieve far more than we imagined possible. We also learn and improve the skills we need to prosper in today's tough competitive environment. Chapter 4 explores the link between learning and stretch goals and explains how you can use outcome-based goals to drive and respond to change. A series of specific tools is provided in Chapter 4 that expands on the idea of stretch. These tools will help you inject creative and personal tension into your goals.

Chapters 5 and 6 introduce you to the concept of *working arenas* and describe how you can match performance goals to working arenas in order to avoid the chaos that too often troubles today's organizations. Instead of hopelessly trying to make all your goals fit your job, Chapter 5 encourages you to identify the working arenas you contribute to, and then fit outcome-based goals to those arenas. Chapter 6 helps you use working arenas to align and coordinate goals throughout the organization. In Chapter 6, you will learn why a single, all-purpose, static picture of organizational alignment is impossible in today's fast-moving world. But you will also learn how to dynamically align your organization around the visions, strategies, initiatives, and directions that matter most to customers, shareholders, and the people of your enterprise.

Chapter 7 concludes the book's focus on aligning and coordinating performance goals. It more fully discusses the cycle of sustainable performance introduced in Chapter 1. In Chapter 7, you will learn how to link goals that primarily matter to customers to goals that primarily matter to shareholders to goals that primarily matter to the people of your enterprise and their partners. There are leading and lagging, cause-and-effect relationships among goals at all levels of the organization. By understanding these lead/lag relationships and by identifying whether the time frames to complete goals are simultaneous or sequential, you can make sense out of all the various performance challenges and goals in your organization.

Chapters 8 through 10 review the management disciplines you must use to achieve the outcome-based performance goals you set. Chapter 8 concentrates on the two essential disciplines by which small groups achieve performance: the team discipline and the working group discipline. Each of these is good. The issue of which to use is not an idealistic or moral choice of "command and control" versus "engage and empower." Rather, the question for any small group is which discipline makes the most sense in light of each specific performance goal the group faces. Chapter 8 describes how your small group can use a *performance agenda* to identify the most critical goals to pursue, and to choose when to use the team discipline versus the working group discipline to accomplish those goals.

Chapter 9 describes the difference between managing horizontally across processes and managing vertically in functions. Again, each of these disciplines is important; the question is which discipline best achieves the goals at hand. Chapter 9 reviews the familiar particulars for managing functionally. It also describes the management principles to use when you face a horizontal process performance challenge. Finally, Chapter 10 reviews the management disciplines you must understand in order to succeed in the face of change. It introduces you to the critical distinction between decision-driven change and behavior-driven change, and describes how to manage each successfully.

Chapter 11 concludes the book with a step-by-step design for building an outcomes management system in your organization. By using the design explained in Chapter 11 (as supplemented by the frameworks, tools, and techniques described throughout the book), you can ensure that your entire organization and everyone in it are managing for performance.

Mindbook and Workbook Sections

The challenge of setting and achieving performance goals differs dramatically today from what it was 30 years ago. Nevertheless, many of our deepest managerial instincts and practices were established in the 1950s and 1960s. You can rid yourself of this cumbersome heritage if you work to understand and use the concepts, frameworks, tools, and techniques in this book. To help you, I have included both explanatory Mindbook sections and practice Workbook sections in each chapter.

Mindbook: In the Mindbook sections, you will find descriptions and explanations for key concepts, frameworks, tools, and techniques, as well as the specific obstacles and difficulties that get in the way of using them. The Mindbook sections seek to build your intellectual understanding of how to set and achieve the performance goals that matter.

Workbook: The Workbook sections include exercises you and your colleagues can use to practice the concepts, frameworks, tools, and techniques. By using the Workbook exercises, you can convert understanding into action, and action into results.

The Mindbook and Workbook sections will reward you most if you use them with specific reference to a particular performance challenge you currently face at work. This is not hard to do. All of you are contributing to many specific performance challenges. For example, as you read these words you might be contributing to a quality initiative. Or you might be implementing a new marketing strategy. Or you might be reengineering a critical process. Or you might be working with a strategic vendor or partner to explore more effective ways to collaborate. Or you might be developing plans for better serving one or more customers or customer segments. Or you might be designing and building information technology that will enable people in your organization to become much more effective.

Take a moment right now and set forth one to five specific performance challenges that most concern you. Use the following space to write these down (in pencil!):

———————————————————————————————

———————————————————————————————

———————————————————————————————

———————————————————————————————

———————————————————————————————

As you read and use the Mindbook sections in this book, keep these specific challenges in mind. Importantly, make sure that you refer to these challenges when you and your colleagues do the exercises contained in the Workbook sections.

This introduction started by describing this as a how-to book. It ends by claiming that *Make Success Measurable* is also a practical guidebook to thriving in today's fast-moving world. By learning to master the disciplines needed to set and achieve performance, you will guarantee yourself a lifetime of opportunity and achievement. The time has come for all of us to step out of the chaos of activity-based objectives, unconnected and poorly communicated initiatives that promote change for the sake of change, flavor-of-the-month fads, financial goals that are not balanced with concerns for customers and the people of the enterprise, and destructive we-versus-they attitudes and behaviors that build cynicism and despair. You don't need to be a victim of this disarray. Instead, you can lead yourself and others into a world of organization performance characterized by goals that are outcomes; goals that are clear, specific, and coordinated; and goals that drive you and others to learn the skills and disciplines needed for success that matters to customers, shareholders and funders, and yourselves. You only need to let measurable success and performance show you the way.

CHAPTER 1

Focus on Outcomes, Not Activities

MIND BOOK

Using Outcomes, Not Activities, as Goals

Performance begins with focusing on outcomes instead of activities. In my experience, most people in most organizations most of the time do the reverse. They concentrate their efforts on the pursuit of activities instead of outcomes. As a result, they rarely set or achieve performance results that matter.

If you read the goals of many people, you will see comments such as "research what customers want," "develop plans to reduce errors," "reorganize into teams," "improve cross-functional communication," and "reengineer our costs." These are not effective performance goals. They are activities that may or may not produce performance results that matter. For example, "research what customers want" is an activity that might lead to improvements in meeting customer needs. And "develop plans to reduce errors" is an activity that might lead to fewer errors. But neither of these activities lets the people involved know when they have succeeded, or even how their efforts matter to their own success and that of their organizations.

Some activity-based goals are even worse than something like "research what customers want." Consider "improve cross-functional communication." Good cross-functional communication is one of many characteristics of effective organizations. But this goal tells us nothing about performance outcomes that matter. If you were part of a group pursuing this goal, you would know neither why you were working to improve cross-functional communication nor how to evaluate whether you had succeeded.

Regrettably, activity-based goals too often produce dispiriting experiences and mediocrity in organizational life. When people lack the most basic understanding of why their efforts matter and how to recognize success, the self-confident spirit of a high-performance organization evaporates. People throughout the organization seek refuge in the pursuit of activities without any clear purpose. "We" are always trying our best to research what customers want, develop plans to reduce errors, reorganize into teams, improve cross-functional communication, and reengineer our costs. But "they" are never putting forth a best effort. "They" are forever getting in the way of . . . of what, exactly? "We" are not too sure. But when it comes time to review our performance, "we" can point to any number of activities we have undertaken to, for example, research customer needs. "We" have done our best, and no one can convince us otherwise. "They" had better reward us. And if the organization continues to flounder? Well, hey, "we" feel bad about it, but it's not our fault. "We've" done our job.

Don't let yourself drift into waters like these. Don't waste your working life pursuing activities for the sake of activities. Instead, begin your journey toward performance by focusing on outcomes and results that matter instead of activities only. If you prefer, instead of *outcomes* you can choose any of the following words: *impacts, consequences, ends, effects,* or *payoffs*. Or you can choose any other word—*so long as the clear and easily grasped meaning of that word is the performance outcome or result of effort instead of a description of the effort itself.*

For example, consider the word *payoff*. Will you and others quickly and dependably interpret *payoff* to mean the impacts, outcomes, and results you hope will happen instead of only the activities by which you conduct that effort? If yes, then go ahead and use the word *payoff*. Otherwise, avoid it.

Notice, please, I am not saying that activities are bad; I am saying that goals that are *activity-based* are ineffective. Activities are the things people must do to produce performance outcomes. We cannot achieve outcomes without doing activities. As Figure 1.1 illustrates, activities are the inputs by which we achieve the impacts of performance results.

But activities are not outcomes. When people confuse activities with goals, they get lost. They soon cease all pursuit of clear and compelling outcomes and results. They travel in circles. Instead of producing outcomes that matter, activity-based goals only produce more activities that in turn produce still more activities, and so on. In contrast, when people have clear, outcome-based performance goals, they know best how to choose, conduct, evaluate,

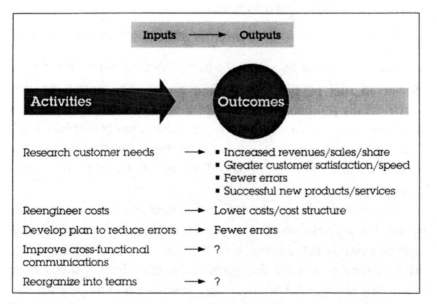

FIGURE 1.1 Are your goals activity-based or outcome-based?

and modify the activities necessary for such achievement. They continue to do activities, but with clear purposes and goals in mind.

Let me illustrate this in the context of team performance. Since the publication of Jon Katzenbach's and my book, *The Wisdom of Teams* (Harvard Business School Press, 1993), I have had the opportunity to observe thousands of team-oriented efforts in organizations. Sometimes the context has been a single, small group. Other times it has been many small groups spanning the organization. I always ask those involved, "What are the performance outcomes you are trying to achieve?" Far too often, people describe the activities associated with teaming instead of the results such teaming might accomplish:

"We need to work collaboratively."

"We need to be a team."

"We're trying to make sure all relevant functions participate."

"We want to have more teams."

"We're reorganizing into teams."

"We need to make sure everyone gets trained in how to team."

Are such activities helpful? Most of the time, yes. But I have observed that people who participate in such initiatives only accidentally produce performance results that matter. They lack the most basic sense of what they are trying to accomplish. Look back at the responses. Not a word in them tells you *why* all the collaboration, multifunctional effort, teaming, and training matters to performance.

The least likely way to deliver team performance is to make your primary objective "becoming a team." Yet each of the activity-based answers listed above has "becoming a team" as the objective lurking at or near the surface. People who are focused on "working more collaboratively" or "ensuring that all perspectives are present" or "increasing the number of teams" are people trying to be a team as opposed to people seeking to apply the team discipline to deliver specific performance outcomes and results that matter.

Clear and compelling performance objectives are the driving force behind teams, not the desire to be a team. Teams that understand the difference between outcomes and activities are teams that are well positioned to learn the discipline needed to perform. (See Chapter 8 for an overview of the team discipline.) Examples of such team performance outcomes include:

- Win contracts from at least two major equipment manufacturers based on our new component design by the end of this calendar year.

- Have five joint local/national headquarters fund-raising teams succeed in raising at least $100,000 each from new sources over the next 15 months.

- Within 60 days, deliver to senior management specific recommendations, which, if implemented, could cut new product development time in half, while simultaneously doubling our commercial success rate.

- Never permit any customer checkout line to be more than three people long.

- By May 15, eliminate our delivery backlog entirely, while also meeting all current deliveries in under 48 hours.

There is a night-and-day difference between these clear and compelling outcome-based performance goals and the activity-based goals stated earlier. Most people most of the time are far more likely to achieve performance results *and* learn the team discipline if they have outcome-based performance goals instead of activity-based goals.

The same is true for other critical skill, behavior, and working relationship challenges beyond teaming. By focusing on performance outcomes and results instead of activities, people throughout today's organizations can master challenges ranging from improved customer service, quality, supplier partnering, strategic alliances, and innovation to reengineering, core competencies, and continuous improvement. Unfortunately, far too many people in for-profit, nonprofit, and governmental organizations, whether in executive offices or at the front lines, are focused on activities instead of outcomes.

Don't make this mistake. Setting and achieving results that matter begin with outcome-based goals instead of activity-based goals. The following Mindbook and Workbook sections will help you and your colleagues make this shift from activities to results. The first section explains why an orientation toward performance results has become so challenging. Understanding these difficulties can help you avoid them. The second section provides exercises you can use to set outcome-based goals instead of activity-based goals.

Why an Orientation toward Outcomes Has Become Rare

The majority of people know that their organizations must perform and that they must contribute to that performance. This knowledge is as deep-seated as common sense itself. Indeed, I can happily report that I have never (seriously, *never*) heard any objections from any person or group at any level in any kind of organization when I have pointed out the importance of focusing on performance. It is reassuring that all of us know just how fundamentally important an orientation toward performance is.

Paradoxically, however, a routine habit of setting and achieving performance outcomes that matter has become rare. Not (as I have just noted) because people disagree or fail to grasp the importance of performance. Rather, our current activity-oriented habits emerge from a mixture of misguided assumptions, natural human anxieties, and the strong legacy of financial measurement. Meanwhile, as our performance attitudes and skills have weakened, a remarkably new and different set of performance challenges has arisen to confront us. Simply put, we know performance is essential, but we are out of practice and faced with many new performance realities.

Misguided Assumptions

A series of flawed beliefs causes people to assume performance outcomes exist when, in fact, they don't. In an all too typical experience, I once challenged the hundred top executives of a multinational corporation to take some time and come back with statements of "the most critical performance outcomes they and their people were aspiring to achieve." Many of these men and women were so upset about being asked to work on such a basic question that they complained to the CEO and senior vice president of human resources. In both verbal and body language, the complaining executives betrayed all of the assumptions that get in the way of focusing on performance outcomes instead of activities.

- *"I already know that!"* This is the most naked of the misguided assumptions. While I have found it expressed by all manner of jobholders, it is, understandably, particularly characteristic of bosses. Whether senior executives or frontline supervisors, bosses are deeply aware that they are *supposed* to know the performance outcomes that matter most. It is a core part of their job. Consequently, they can be offended by the suggestion that they don't.

- *"The performance outcomes are implied!"* This is a variation on "I already know that!" Consider how fundamentally aware most of us are about performance as the necessary engine of organizational and personal success. It is only a short leap from this most basic belief to the assumption, "Of course the performance outcomes are there! Otherwise, why would we be doing all these activities?" Unfortunately, far too often the performance outcomes are *not* there; they are neither implied by nor easily understood within the activity-based goals spread throughout the organization.

- *"They're in the plans!"* This is a variation on "The performance outcomes are implied!" It is one aspect of the strong legacy of financial measurement we will discuss later. Interestingly, it suggests a kind of alchemist's faith. We are not certain how our activity-based goals (e.g., "improving cross-functional communications") relate to the financial targets stated in this year's budgets and plans. But we take it on faith that, through the alchemy of organization, such activities will be converted into gold! (In a second prevalent version of this, we do not have such faith. Instead, we know for certain that the only goals that matter are the financial results in the plan. Consequently, we ignore—even scorn—goals such as "improve cross-functional coordination" as so much fluff and nice talk.)

- *"That's someone else's job!"* Again, a variation. After all, classically it *was* the job of the boss or the finance group to set goals. But this passive, "somebody else's job" perspective doesn't work in today's fast-paced environment. Yes, bosses and financial people still must set performance directions. *But so must everyone else.* People who assume that their activity-based goals somehow contribute to performance outcomes being set by other people, and yet remain unclear about those outcomes or the connection, are people who are flying blind.

When the CEO and SVP of human resources read the performance goals handed in by the hundred executives, they were shocked. Notwithstanding all the complaints and protests, *less than 10 out of more than 1,000* goal statements set forth real performance outcomes that mattered—Ninety-nine percent of the goal statements were activity-based.

Natural Human Anxieties

Let's face it. Most of us most of the time get nervous when we start to discuss the outcomes by which our success or achievement might be measured. Most of us find it easier and more reassuring to commit to goals entirely within our control and comfort zone. Activity-based goals, then, are the very thing for us. Consider the following goals set by the executives in this story:

- Develop a strategic plan for each of my four markets.
- Hold quarterly reviews with key contributors, beginning second quarter next year.
- Assess whether to expand or exit product line Y.
- Send staff meeting memos to all employees each month.

Each of the executives could easily accomplish each of these goals. And yet, every one of these activity-based goals begs critical questions: Why do these activities matter? How would you know they made any difference to performance? Consider the last of these examples: "Send staff meeting memos to all employees each month." Undoubtedly, the executive in this case wanted to keep the people in her division better informed about the direction and decisions emerging from staff meetings. All of us should applaud this. But how would the executive know she had succeeded? What is the outcome this executive should target as the result—the real performance purpose—of employee involvement and understanding?

It is not easy to state goals and outcomes for such things as employee involvement and understanding. However, seeking refuge in pure and easily accomplished activities is an unconstructive response to this dilemma. Indeed, activity-based goals like those listed above are shams, and we know it.

The basic anxiety and risk aversion most of us feel about setting real outcomes as goals—let alone stretch outcomes—will always be around, particularly when new and different challenges confront us. The central question is whether we will allow the anxiety to control us, or will we control our anxiety?

The Legacy of Financial Measurement

Ask how to evaluate the performance of an enterprise and invariably the answer comes dressed in financial terms such as revenues, costs, and profits. This should surprise no one. Organizations have measured and evaluated their performance financially as long as any of us can remember. And we have become very sophisticated at doing so. Simple balance sheet and profit-and-loss indicators of the early twentieth century have evolved into a complex array of financial indicators including share price, earnings per share, cash flows, coverage, and other ratios. This financial orientation is an integral part of our everyday experience and reality. It is even embedded in our language. The phrase most often used to describe performance is "the bottom line."

Our sophisticated financial orientation has bestowed tremendous economic value upon our organizations and ourselves. Nothing that follows is meant to suggest that we abandon this perspective. Having said and meant that, however, we have reached a point in history when an *exclusively* financial approach to organization performance no longer works. Indeed, even today's most astute financial executives recognize that the financial-only approach is self-defeating. The surest way to ruin financial measures, they will tell you, is by focusing only on financial measures. More and more leaders today call for a balanced scorecard that recognizes the necessity of delivering performance to all of the stakeholders who matter to the health of the enterprise (see Figure 1.2).

As balanced scorecards get introduced, however, most organizations quickly discover just how iron-fisted is the grip of the orientation toward financial results. This should not surprise us. We should never underestimate the power a financial perspective has on our lives. Today, the assertion that financial indicators no longer occupy the fixed center of our performance universe is as

	For-profit enterprise	Nonprofit enterprise	Governmental enterprise
Always	Customers People of the enterprise Shareholders	Beneficiaries/customers People of the enterprise Donors/funders	Beneficiaries/citizens People of the enterprise Taxpayers/citizens
Sometimes	Alliance partners Regulators Communities	Alliance partners Regulators Communities	Alliance partners Future Generations

FIGURE 1.2 Stakeholders (constituencies) who matter to the sustainable health of the enterprise.

heretical as Copernicus's sixteenth-century refutation of Ptolemy. Ptolemy's system had governed the learned mind for *1,400 years*. It took several hundred more years before most people *believed* Ptolemy was mistaken. Hopefully, it will not take as long for people to believe—*really believe*—there is more to performance than financial results.

To help you and your colleagues along the way toward a more balanced view of performance, let me point out three particular pitfalls of the financial-only perspective.

Pitfall No. 1: Unsustainability

As mentioned, a singular obsession with financial indicators ultimately destroys those indicators. Figure 1.3 illustrates why. Achieving sustained organizational performance demands outcomes and results that benefit all of the constituencies that matter. It also demands that the outcomes beneficial to any single constituency actually fuel or reinforce the outcomes beneficial to others. Thus, the balanced performance orientation in Figure 1.3 reads as follows: "Shareholders who provide opportunities and rewards to people of the enterprise to deliver value to customers who generate returns to shareholders who provide opportunities to people of the enterprise, and so on." In governmental or nonprofit organizations, the same reinforcing cycle obtains, although

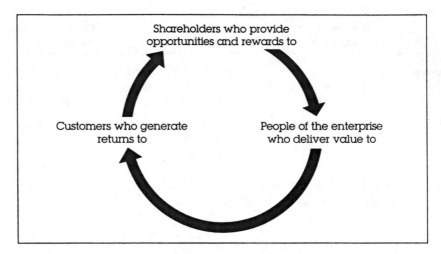

FIGURE 1.3 The cycle of sustainable performance.

"shareholders" are replaced by "citizens/taxpayers" (governments) or "donors/supporters" (nonprofits); and "customers" are replaced by "beneficiaries and customers."

A strict financial-only performance perspective inevitably ignores or undervalues the other constituencies. As organization after organization has discovered to its dismay, this narrow view results in poor customer service, shoddy products, unfulfilled and unhappy people in the enterprise, and other cancerous phenomena, all of which eventually reflect themselves in poor numbers. The wisest executives understand that financial indicators are lagging; that is, they are the effect caused by other leading indicators such as customer satisfaction and people's skills or competencies. A balanced performance orientation, then, is one that includes but goes beyond financial indicators only. Whether considering the entire organization, a business unit within the organization, a function or department, a key cross-functional process, a team, or a single person's contribution, sustainable performance emerges when we move beyond the financial-only legacy we have inherited to a richer variety of reinforcing performance outcomes and results (see Figure 1.4).

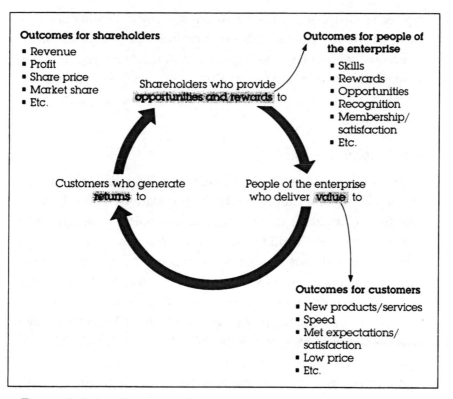

Outcomes for shareholders
- Revenue
- Profit
- Share price
- Market share
- Etc.

Shareholders who provide opportunities and rewards to

Outcomes for people of the enterprise
- Skills
- Rewards
- Opportunities
- Recognition
- Membership/ satisfaction
- Etc.

Customers who generate returns to

People of the enterprise who deliver value to

Outcomes for customers
- New products/services
- Speed
- Met expectations/ satisfaction
- Low price
- Etc.

FIGURE 1.4 Reinforcing performance outcomes.

Pitfall No. 2: Demotivation

Today's challenging world demands tremendous energy and enthusiasm from people throughout the organization. Financial goals typically inspire only the narrow few (e.g., senior executives) instead of the broad many (all of the people of the enterprise). Yes, financial outcomes should and do energize top executives as well as partners in professional service firms. Why? Because such people either are, or are rewarded as if they were, owners. In addition, financial goals classically motivate people whose work directly contributes to financial results—for example, people in sales and marketing. Finally, during periods of rapid growth or imminent decline (such as pending bankruptcy), financial goals can inspire the entire organization. Beyond such people or situations, however, financial-only indicators are most often music to deaf ears. The vast majority of people simply do not *hear* them. In fact, such goals can demotivate people if they suspect their leaders care more about self-enrichment than about delivering value to customers and building prosperity and opportunity for all.

Pitfall No. 3: Confusion

Perhaps the most recognizable defect of financial-only goals is the barrier that inevitably blocks the translation of overall corporate financial goals into subgoals that people in the enterprise can pursue with confidence. Consider revenue, profitability, share price, and market share goals. At the top of an organization, such goals make sense because the CEO and his or her direct reports can understand how the entire organization might work together to accomplish them. Yet, when senior executives begin to dissect such goals into subgoals for the third, fourth, fifth, and lower levels of the organization, they run into trouble. Yes, they can give revenue or share goals to sales and marketing people, and they can give cost goals to everyone. But that's it. What top executives see as a rich mixture of organization effort becomes a thin gruel for everyone else. Again, refer to Figure 1.4. People throughout the organization need to set and achieve performance results across the spectrum, not just the single strand of revenue (e.g., sales) or cost (e.g., operations) that seems relevant to their function. When top management's overall financial goals do not translate into such meaningful contributions, people get confused about how and why their contribution makes a difference. In the midst of such confusion, people often resort to setting activity-based goals.

When combined, these misguided assumptions, natural anxieties, and the strong financial legacy help explain why people find it so difficult to focus on performance outcomes instead of activities. As you reflect on your own performance challenges, you should be candid about such obstacles. Having done that, the most important step you and your colleagues can take is to resolve not to allow such forces to get in your way. You can start today. Pick a performance challenge that matters, and work together to identify the performance outcomes and results that make sense to pursue. Yes, of course, identify the activities necessary to accomplish these outcomes. But do not confuse activities with outcomes. The next section provides a series of exercises that you can use to make this all-important shift from a focus on activities to a focus on outcomes.

Consider any effort, initiative, program, plan, assignment, or project to which you are making a contribution. Take a few moments and write a description of that effort and estimate the expected time frame for its completion. Also, identify who else is joining you in the effort. Consider doing the exercises below together with those colleagues. Please note that the exercises employ a variety of different approaches. You may find some more useful than others. Consider practicing all of them until you know which work best for you.

Exercise 1.1: Mirror, Mirror

Gather any formal goals that you have written down or that are part of your management system. If any or all of you have no written goals at all, discuss the implications of that among yourselves and then move on to Exercise 1.2. If you do have written goals, analyze them. Are they activity-based or outcome-based?

Exercise 1.2: How Would You Know Success?

Imagine that I have just spent 15 to 20 minutes with you and your colleagues. You have explained to me an effort that you have under way and the time frame projected to complete it. Now take 5 or 10 minutes alone, or in pairs, to answer the following question:

> *How would I know if you and your colleagues were successful in this effort?*

In other words, if I were to disappear and return at some relevant point in the future, how would I know whether the effort succeeded? What would you and your colleagues point to as indicators of that success?

Exercise 1.3: The Five Hows

This is a variant on Exercise 1.2 and it comes from a very useful technique called the Five Whys, which helps people gain clarity about why they are doing something. The objective here is to gain increasing clarity and specificity about the performance outcomes that matter most to the effort you and your colleagues have under way.

The exercise starts the same way as Exercise 1.2. Once you have recorded your responses to the question, "How would you know success?," ask the same question again, but with reference to the answers. Continue to do this up to five times, or until your answers describe performance outcomes or results instead of activities. Figure 1.5 illustrates this exercise for the challenge of innovation. Please compare the specificity of the fifth answer with the specificity of the first answer. The fifth answer is a much better outcome-based goal than the first.

Exercise 1.4: Stakeholder/Constituency Analysis

A useful way to gain an outcome focus is to ask yourselves, "To whom does this effort matter, and why?" This basic question guides you toward a performance orientation. Thus, consider the following constituencies that might matter to the success of your organization:

- *External constituencies:* Customers, shareholders, strategic partners, distributors, suppliers, regulators, others.

- *Internal constituencies:* People in other functions, departments, processes; bosses; subordinates, team members; task forces or committees; others.

Whether your effort spans much or all of your organization (e.g., implementing a new strategy) or is confined to yourself and/or a small number of colleagues (e.g., increasing the productivity with which your small group answers customer service calls), take the time to respond to the following three questions:

WORKBOOK

Challenge: Innovation

1. How would you know success?

   Answer: We would do a better job of leading the market.

2. How would you know you succeeded at leading the market?

   Answer: We would be faster at identifying and meeting new customer needs.

3. How would you know you succeeded at being faster at identifying and meeting new customer needs?

   Answer: We would reduce the time it takes us to introduce new products and increase the commercial success rate of those new products.

4. How would you know you succeeded at reducing the time it takes to introduce new products and increase the commercial success rate of those new products?

   Answer: We will cut the time from idea to product introduction in half while doubling the commercial success rate of new products.

5. How would you know you succeeded at cutting the time frame idea to product introduction in half while doubling the commercial success rate of new products?

   Answer: For the next 10 ideas that get the go-ahead, we will take no more than 3 months to introduce each and at least 4 of them will be commercially successful 1 year after their introduction.

FIGURE 1.5 The Five Hows.

1. To which of these constituencies does your effort matter or make a difference?

2. Why does it matter to them? Why do they care?

3. How would they (members of the constituencies) judge whether your effort succeeded?

Exercise 1.5: Scratching the Activity Itch

Okay. Go ahead. Scratch that activity itch! Take some time and list all the activities that you and your colleagues need to complete as part of your effort. That's right. Get them all out on the table. When the frenzy is over, when you feel you've listed all the necessary activities, then go back to Exercise 1.2 or 1.3. With respect to each of these activities, ask, "How would I (or you) know if these activities were successful?"

Exercise 1.6: Metrics/Yardsticks

Take 5 to 10 minutes to identify as many metrics or yardsticks by which you might evaluate the success of your effort. Remember to identify both financial and nonfinancial yardsticks. Having done so, and discussed these yardsticks among yourselves, return to Exercise 1.2.

Exercise 1.7: Inputs—Impacts—Outputs

This exercise is a bit more sophisticated. As illustrated in Figure 1.1, activities are the inputs by which we achieve the outputs of performance outcomes. However, sometimes there is an *intermediate* set of accomplishments that interposes itself between activities and results. Figure 1.6 shows these intermediate accomplishments as *impacts*. You and your colleagues might find it useful to set goals that include a mixture of impacts and outputs.

To illustrate this, consider some of the inputs, impacts, and outputs typically involved in a total quality effort. As shown in Figure 1.6, inputs, or raw activities, almost always include training or education efforts to introduce people to the philosophy and tools of total quality. These inputs lead to intermediate impacts that might include the number of people trained or, even better, the number of teams that have set total quality goals that matter. But the most critical performance outcomes would include the outputs accomplished by those teams, such as errors reduced, cycle times shortened, customer satisfaction increased, revenues gained, and skills learned and applied.

You and your colleagues might find the distinctions among inputs, impacts, and outputs helpful. Accordingly, take time to complete the following table:

WORKBOOK

Inputs (activities) →	Impacts →	Outputs (outcomes)
Train people in the philosophy and tools of total quality.	Number of total quality action teams who have set outcome-based quality goals	Reduced errors Increased customer satisfaction People of the enterprise who have successfully applied total quality

FIGURE 1.6 Inputs—impacts—outputs.

To succeed at our challenge, we need to pay attention to:

Inputs (activities) →	Impacts →	Outputs (outcomes)

Exercises 1.2 through 1.6 will provide you with plenty of material for completing this table. Once you have done so, try crafting one or more outcome-based goals that draw from the second and third columns. The key, as always, is to avoid goals that are entirely activity-based (inputs).

CHAPTER 2

Pick Relevant Metrics

Choosing Metrics That Fit the Challenge

Once you are focused on outcomes instead of activities, the next step to performance is selecting metrics relevant to the challenge at hand. The good news is that, using Chapter 1, you and your colleagues have described the performance outcome(s) you aspire to achieve. Now you need to specify the metrics by which you will assess your success, as well as how much of a difference you seek to achieve and by when.

Sometimes metrics are obvious, although, even then, there are important nuances. Other times, the best measures seem elusive. Consider, for example, a fellow who is overweight and feeling tired and stressed out. One day, this friend tells you he is going on a diet. Knowing the importance of focusing on outcomes instead of activities, you point out that dieting is an activity and ask your friend, "How would you know your diet was successful?" The response is, "I'll lose weight and feel better."

"Terrific!," you say. Now you suggest to him the power of getting specific. He has no problem getting specific about the first outcome he seeks (lose weight). With some thought and determination, he tells you, "I'll take off 15 pounds!" So far, so good.

Still, there are nuances. You can help your friend become even more specific by noting two points—one obvious, the other not. First, you ask, "By when?" He responds, "In two months." Second, you suggest that taking weight off is only the critical first step in a weight loss program. "But," you query, "what about keeping it off?" So, with your help, your friend has a relatively straightforward and specific outcome: *"I'll lose 15 pounds in two months and keep it off for at least three months."*

Your friend can now benefit from the well-known advantages of pursuing performance outcomes with relevant and specific metrics:

- *Tracking:* With the assistance of a weight scale, he can track progress against the goal of losing 15 pounds in the first two months and keeping it off in the following three. Absent the metric of pounds and the specific goal of 15, he would have no idea what to track.

- *Learning:* He can learn which weight-loss activities make the biggest difference. Such learning is as simple as observing cause and effect. As he eats less, eats more wisely, and exercises more, he can observe the connections between such efforts and the weight loss being tracked. By doing so, he can emphasize the dieting and exercise activities that are most effective for him and discontinue those that don't work.

- *Motivation:* His specific goal can fuel his effort with will and determination. Armed with a specific objective, he can convert his anxieties ("I don't know if I can really do this") into the focus and discipline that motivates success ("I *will* take and keep this weight off!").

So far, you have helped your friend a lot. But what about his other desired outcome—to feel better? In contrast to the outcome "lose weight," "feel better" is not so easily measured. "Feel better" is certainly an outcome, not an activity. But how would your friend know if he succeeded? Unlike pounds for weight loss, no obvious and universally accepted yardstick suggests itself. Do not, however, let him give up.

Indeed, in only a short time of creative brainstorming, you and your friend can generate several effective ways to measure success at feeling better. Your friend might seek to lower his blood pressure or to achieve a certain heart rate following a stress test or some particular form of exercise. Your friend might set specific goals to eliminate or reduce consumption of items such as cigarettes, alcohol, or coffee with well-established links to stress. He might choose an exercise such as bicycling or running and set a related performance goal (*"I'll run five miles every day and reduce my time by 15 percent within six weeks"*). Your friend might seek to attain one or more moments of well-being on a daily basis and keep a diary as a means to monitor his performance against that goal. Or he might set a goal that requires a spouse or colleague at work to help him monitor (*"Within a month, I will reduce the number of times I am short-tempered at work from several times a day to no more than once a week, and, within two months, I will reduce it to zero"*).

When it comes to picking relevant metrics, many of today's most pressing organization performance challenges are more like "feel better" than like "lose weight." Consider, for example, delivering total customer satisfaction, being customer-driven, achieving total quality, having the most respected brand, partnering with others, being the fastest, being the preferred provider, being the most innovative, having the best place to work, having one or more world-class competencies, being truly global or transnational or transcultural or diverse, and building one firm. These challenges demand attention to more than the financial and economic metrics with which we are so familiar. Yes, there certainly is a link between success with such challenges and profits, revenues, costs, and market share. But, as Chapter 1 pointed out, profit, revenue, cost, and market share goals too often fail to effectively capture the full purpose of many of today's critical aspirations—just as weight loss is an incomplete way to help your friend feel better. Like the dieting friend who wants to feel better, you and your colleagues must contend with a series of difficulties in trying to pick relevant and specific metrics.

There Is No Metric Universally Recognized as Effective

Weight itself, as measured in pounds or kilos, is universally accepted as an effective measure of weight loss. Similarly, revenues, profits, and market share are universally recognized as effective metrics of competitive superiority and financial performance. But no universally recognized metrics have emerged for such challenges as customer satisfaction, quality, partnering with others, being the preferred provider, innovation, and being the best place to work. Just like your friend who wants to feel better, you and your colleagues must find and use performance metrics that make sense. You must avoid getting stuck as the result of the absence of a universally recognized yardstick.

Some Criteria Are Quantitative and Objective; Others Are Qualitative and Subjective

If your friend sets a performance goal of eliminating cigarettes entirely, he can monitor progress easily because the metric is quantitative and objective. But what about the goal to have one or more moments of well being on a daily basis? As you know, stress-free people regularly experience such moments. Thus, it is a performance outcome that is both specific and assessable. Using a diary, your friend can track progress and learn from such a goal. Still, this kind of outcome is far more qualitative than quantitative, and more subjective than objective. Candor and honesty are required for your friend to effectively use this metric because, otherwise, progress toward his goal is too easily manipulated.

Now, consider a company's aspiration to build partnering relationships with key suppliers or customers. On the one hand, establishing certain threshold goals about the amount of business conducted with each potential partner can provide quantitative and objective performance outcomes. On the other hand, the company and the supplier or customer might meet such criteria and still not have a true partnering relationship. Typically, partnership implies a variety of subjective and qualitative characteristics. For example, partners trust one another, regularly consult with one another on critical matters, share highly confidential information with one another, and seek out each other before anyone else regarding new opportunities and challenges. Yet, as with moments of well being, setting and achieving performance outcomes related to phenomena such as trust demand candor and honesty in order to benefit from tracking, learning, and motivation. It is perfectly okay to use such qualitative and subjective criteria; indeed, sometimes they are the best, most accurate reflection of the performance challenge at hand. But you must recognize and then surmount the difficulties in doing so.

Many Metrics Require Extra Work and Effort

Obviously, criteria that are subjective and qualitative (such as your friend's moments of well-being or your company's number of partnering relationships) demand more work and effort to monitor than familiar goals such as weight loss or revenues, profits, and market share. Quantitative and objective performance outcomes that are new or novel also can demand extra work. For example, in your friend's case, the use of heart rate as a metric for feeling better is both objective and quantitative. But it also demands extra work and effort because your friend probably does not currently monitor his heart rate following exercise. Similarly, an organization's goal to be the fastest, say, at product delivery can be measured objectively in terms of speed or cycle time. But it demands extra work and effort. The organization must pick a starting point (perhaps when the customer places the order), an ending point (perhaps when the customer takes delivery of the order), and put in place the processes and practices needed to regularly and effectively measure time or speed. Do not let the burden of extra work prevent you from using a new metric that best fits the challenge before you.

If You Have Never Used a Chosen Metric Before, There Will Be No Baseline

Once again, consider an organization's desire to be the fastest at product delivery. If the organization has never monitored the speed of the process from order generation through delivery, people in the organization will have no preexisting baseline against which to pick specific goals and outcomes for improvement. In situations like this, the parties involved might throw up their hands and ask, "How can we set a goal if we don't know how we're doing now?" It is an understandable question. Yet, a moment's reflection indicates that people and organizations would *never* move beyond yesterday's metrics if the absence of a baseline for a new metric were seen as fatal. Instead, you must rely on gut feel and whatever indicators you have to pick an outcome-based goal and then use your performance against that outcome to drive improvement as well as to set the baseline for future goals and performance.

Some Criteria Demand Contributions from People Who May Not Be Subject to Your Control or Authority

When your friend seeks the specific performance outcome of increasing the moments of well-being at work, he depends on the participation of other people. For example, his boss might have certain habits or behaviors that trigger stress. Without obtaining a shift in behavior from his boss, your friend is less likely to achieve the performance outcome he seeks. He would do well, therefore, to share his goal with his boss and other colleagues at work, and to ask for their support and help. However, your friend cannot command that help.

The same principle applies to many of today's performance challenges that require contributions from different departments or functions or silos. For example, the performance outcome of building the most respected brand requires much more than effective advertising. Organizations such as Coca-Cola, McDonald's, Nike, and the American Red Cross have respected brands because those brands make explicit promises that *the entire organization* effectively and routinely fulfills. For example, the American Red Cross brand communicates a promise of quick, effective, and comprehensive disaster relief that people throughout the Red Cross, not just those in marketing, make a reality. Accordingly, while the marketing people in your organization might aspire to build the most respected brand, they cannot do it themselves. Instead, the specific goals associated with such an effort require contributions from people over whom those in marketing have no direct control or authority. Do not permit your lack of control over other people to prevent you from selecting the metric that best fits your challenge.

Some Metrics Are Leading Indicators of Success; Others Are Lagging Indicators

When your dieting friend sets a goal to exercise regularly, his success is a leading indicator of feeling better. In other words, his success at meeting outcome-based exercise goals *causes* his success at feeling better. Put in the reverse, moments of well-being are a lagging effect of exercise. The central importance of this lead/lag phenomenon is relatively new in the world of organization performance. When financial and market indicators such as profits, revenues, and market share were all that mattered to the bottom line, most people in most organizations had no reason to concern themselves with the lead/lag relationship among their goals.

Today, the performance landscape has shifted. Consider, for example, the aspiration of total customer satisfaction. If your organization delivers total customer satisfaction, can you expect gains in revenue, profit, and market share? Yes. Okay, should you use revenue, profit, and share gains as the goals of customer satisfaction? No.

Why not? Because while revenue, profit, and share gains are a *lagging effect* of customer satisfaction, they are also a lagging effect of other causes (number and strength of competitors, effective purchasing, distribution presence and economics, and so on). Using revenue, profit, market share, and similar metrics as the *sole* measure of everything an organization does may be theoretically possible, but it is pragmatically nonsensical and even nightmarish. No one would know for sure what difference he or she was making. No one would really know whether and to what extent changes in, say, market share were due to shifts in customer satisfaction versus introduction of new products versus distribution strategies versus . . . well, anything and everything the organization is doing. Indeed, as Chapter 1 indicated, this financial-only approach is what most organizations are struggling to shun rather than embrace. Consequently, you and your colleagues must spend time sorting out the lead/lag relationship among the possible metrics you will use. (See Chapter 7 for further discussion of lead/lag relationships.)

Make a Choice and Stick with It Long Enough to Learn

Having too many goals is the same as having no goal at all. A wonderful aspect of your friend's weight loss goal is that it provides laser-like focus that is quantitative, objective, and universally recognized as effective. In contrast, none of the "feel better" goals are nearly so tidy; each has one or more of the faults we have just reviewed. Still, your friend must make a choice. He must select one or two, or maybe three, of the metrics associated with the "feel better" performance outcome. Choosing all of them will not work. Indeed, the greater the number of metrics and goals he pursues, the more likely he is to fall into the trap of losing focus.

This commonsense rule also applies to organizational aspirations such as being the best place to work, being the preferred provider, or being customer-driven. With a bit of effort and creativity, you and your colleagues can brainstorm a list of possible metrics for setting and evaluating progress toward such performance aspirations. But you must avoid pursuing the entire list or even a very large part of it. You must make a choice. You must focus. And you must stick with your choice long enough to gain the benefit of tracking, learning, and motivation. Think what would happen if your dieting friend chose to reduce alcohol consumption, then two weeks later abandoned that in favor of seeking a lower heart rate following exercise, then a week later shifted to increasing his moments of well being. Such skittish inconstancy won't work for your friend, nor will it work for you and your colleagues to shift so easily and often from one set of metrics and goals to another. You must give yourselves a chance to benefit from tracking, learning, and motivation. You must stick with your chosen metrics and goals long enough to learn and progress.

Each of these difficulties generates anxiety and reluctance. And, of course, they compound one another. It is tough enough for your friend to set and stick with a specific goal to lose and keep off 15 pounds. But, it is far more difficult for your friend to establish the resolve—the will—to stick with a choice among the many possible goals and metrics related to feeling better, none of which are universally recognized, and several of which are subjective or qualitative, require extra work to track, or perhaps require the contribution of other people to achieve. Yet your friend must overcome such obstacles if he is to succeed. Similarly, you and your colleagues must summon the determination to work through such worries if you are to learn how to select the metrics that best fit today's most urgent performance challenges. The next section introduces you to four sets of metrics (the *four yardsticks*) that can help you become increasingly comfortable in choosing and sticking with the best measures of progress.

The Four Yardsticks

All performance challenges are measurable by some combination of what I call the *four yardsticks:*

1. Speed/time

2. Cost

3. On-spec/expec quality

4. Positive yields

The first three of these are objective and quantitative; the fourth is a blend of objective and subjective, quantitative and qualitative. If you learn to use the four yardsticks, you can eliminate many of the difficulties and anxieties related to picking the metrics that make a difference in today's most pressing performance challenges.

Speed/Time

Use this yardstick whenever your performance challenge relates to the speed or time it takes for something—typically, a process—to happen. If you and your colleagues are trying to become faster at a process, or if you need to eliminate unnecessary steps, reduce costs, or coordinate the efforts of many people across multiple tasks, then speed and time are powerful metrics to choose. For example, speed and time are critical metrics for any performance challenges that cut across the silos or functions of an organization—challenges such as product or service innovation, time to market, reduction of cycle time, total customer service, and manufacturing and logistics effectiveness. If you have ever reengineered work, you have contended with the challenge of speed and time.

To use speed and time effectively, you and your colleagues must *define the process or series of steps you are measuring.* For example, many of today's organizations work hard to reduce the time it takes from generating customer orders through satisfying those orders. Having named the process, you must then *pick the starting and stopping steps of that process.* As Figures 2.1 through 2.3 illustrate, the starting and stopping steps in this cycle or process can vary—and the difficulty and impact of your challenge can also vary depending on the choices you make. The speed challenge in "receipt of customer order through customer receipt of delivery" (Figure 2.1) is less difficult than "receipt of customer order through customer first use" (Figure 2.2). And "first customer contact through complete customer satisfaction" (Figure 2.3) is the most difficult and comprehensive of all three.

Why? Well, each of the starting and stopping points in Figure 2.1 is objectively identifiable. It is easy to identify the exact points in time when a customer order is received by your company and when the customer receives delivery of your goods. In contrast, the ending point in Figure 2.2 ("customer first use") demands

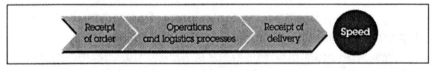

FIGURE 2.1 Receipt of customer order through customer receipt of delivery.

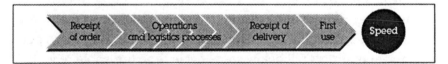

FIGURE 2.2 Receipt of customer order through customer first use.

FIGURE 2.3 First customer contact through complete customer satisfaction.

much more work, requires the cooperation of the customer, and, in the case of software or complicated industrial products, calls for judgment about what constitutes first use. Figure 2.3 adds further complications. By designating "first customer contact" as the initial step, the entire sales process and all of the people included in it have been grafted onto the operations and logistics processes of Figure 2.1. Moreover, "complete customer satisfaction" involves even more steps (e.g., customer service) and adds assessment difficulties (qualitative, subjective metrics; extra work; customer cooperation; no universally recognized yardstick; etc.).

On the other hand, if your organization seeks to be *totally* customer-driven as well as the fastest, Figure 2.3 portrays a far more comprehensive and customer-sensitive process than Figure 2.1. Figure 2.2 depicts a middle ground between the other two. None of these three is necessarily best. The point is that, if you and your colleagues choose time and speed as your metrics, then you also must make choices about the starting and stopping points of the process you will measure—and you must do so in light of the overall performance challenge you are trying to meet.

Next, you must *pick some unit of time* as the specific metric in your performance goal. Will you seek to reduce the cycle time in terms of years, months, weeks, days, hours, minutes, seconds, or fractions of seconds? Moreover, you must *make a choice about number and frequency.* Are you seeking to reduce the average time from receipt of order through receipt of delivery? Or are you seeking to ensure that 100 percent (or some other very high percentage) of orders fall below some cycle time threshold (e.g., 100 percent of orders in less than 24 hours). Finally, you must *make the effort required to measure speed and time.* Having defined the starting and stopping points of what you'll measure as well as the time units, number, and frequency, you must actually do the work of measurement. As you know, this can have implications for information systems as well as people's roles in various parts of the organization.

Figure 2.4 summarizes the choices you must make to use speed and time effectively. By the way, the order-generation through fulfillment processes laid out in Figures 2.1 through 2.3 apply to services as well as products, and to individual consumers as well as commercial customers. For example, these figures pertain as easily to mortgages, haircuts, and lube and oil jobs as to cookies, vacuum cleaners, and automobiles. In business-to-business markets, they describe the order-generation through fulfillment process for maintenance, payroll, consulting, legal, and other services, as well as the sale and delivery of industrial or other kinds of products.

The order-generation through fulfillment process is one of the most fundamental work processes in any organization. Other basic processes include new product/service introduction, customer service, integrated logistics, and hiring, development, and retention of people.

Cost

Of the four yardsticks, this is the most familiar. Most people in organizations have many years of experience attending to cost as

---

1. What is the process or series of work steps you wish to measure?

2. What step starts the clock?

3. What step stops the clock?

4. What unit of time makes the most sense?

5. What number and frequency of items going through the process must meet your speed requirements?

6. What adjustments to roles and resources (e.g., systems) are needed to do the work of measurement and to achieve the goal?

FIGURE 2.4 Speed/time choices.

well as setting and achieving cost goals. Still, there are nuances and choices. First, you must *choose between focusing on units of activity or materials and combinations of units of activities and/or materials.* For most of the twentieth century, organizations focused more on unit costs than on combinations of activities, believing that if each person or department throughout the organization worried about reducing unit costs, then minimal total costs would follow. In this view, cost goals mimicked organization charts—individual unit costs rolled into departmental costs, then into functional costs, then into company costs. *Many challenges still benefit from this view.* For example, it is critical for organizations to work hard to reduce overall purchasing costs, and they can usefully focus on the unit costs of materials purchased to accomplish that.

In the past decade, however, this unit-by-unit view has fallen from favor out of a preference for an activity, or process, view. Today, many of our most significant performance challenges require looking across a combination of different activities to reduce the total cost of that combination—or, put more familiarly, the total cost of that process. Thus, consider again the "receipt of order through receipt of delivery" process shown in Figure 2.1. It is important to recognize that, just as in the case of speed and time, if you seek to reduce the cost of a combination or process, then *you must define the starting point and stopping point of that combination or process.*

In addition, for both traditional unit cost goals and activity or process cost goals, you must *decide whether you will count indirect as well as direct costs and, if so, which indirect costs.* Next, you must *define an allocation method for the indirect costs you wish to count.* Experience suggests that the more direct the relationship between any activity, unit, or material and the object of the costing effort, the easier it is to know what and how to count. For example, the salary, benefits, travel and entertainment, and office support costs associated with a purchasing officer are easily attributed to the materials or services purchased by that officer.

On the other hand, the more indirect and abstract the relationship between a source of cost and the thing (activity, material, or combination) being costed, the more difficult it is to know what and how to count. And the more difficult it is to know what and how to count, the more likely it is that cost allocation schemes are arbitrary. Finally, the more arbitrary the cost allocation scheme, the less likely it is that the allocated costs will benefit from problem-solving techniques.

Let's explore this critical idea. Imagine for a moment that you and your colleagues seek to reduce total purchasing costs for hardware and software. You decide that you will count everything, even such overhead as the salaries and benefits of the CEO, the senior vice president of human resources, and other top executives. Here's what will happen. Because your company's top executives do not dedicate much, if any, time to hardware and software purchasing, you will inevitably pick some completely arbitrary method for assigning some of the top executives' salary and related costs to hardware and software purchasing. The same will happen with many other aspects of overhead. Nevertheless, say you move ahead and succeed in "totally" costing out the purchasing of hardware and software.

Now that you know "total" purchasing cost, you will turn your attention to problem solving in an effort to reduce purchasing costs. As you do, your group will soon discover that you cannot come up with any effective ideas for reducing the costs associated with the top executives and other arbitrarily allocated overhead. Consequently, you will focus your problem-solving efforts on those costs you *can* do something about. And these will largely be costs that are directly associated with purchasing. Put differently, you and your colleagues will treat the CEO-type, arbitrary allocations as a given that cannot be changed. The obvious question is, "Why did you include such allocated amounts in the first place?"

Note the important difference between the pure arbitrariness of allocating CEO time to purchasing hardware and software and the challenge of allocating and assigning total activity or process costs that, while perhaps new to you or others, are not arbitrary. Consider again the goal of reducing the total process cost of "receipt of order through receipt of delivery," shown in Figure 2.1. You and your colleagues would be wise to form a team from operations, customer service, sales, logistics, and finance to tackle this challenge. Each function will contribute relevant knowledge and experience, but each will also bring areas of ignorance. For example, someone from a department that receives customer orders will know little about assigning costs from operations or sales, and vice versa. Just because each person has an area of ignorance, however, does not mean that the *team* is ignorant. On the contrary, by working together, the team can figure out the best way to set, measure, problem-solve, and achieve a cost reduction goal for the whole process.

On-Spec/Expec Quality

This yardstick applies to any performance challenge that demands adherence to one or more specifications (*on spec*) or customer expectations (customer expectations, or "expec" for short). Product and service specifications generally derive from production and operational standards, legal and regulatory requirements, and customer and competitive demands. In this last sense, then, specifications overlap with customer expectations. But, nearly always, there exist customer expectations that exceed the specifications any organization mandates for its products and services. Such expectations reflect an array of customer concerns as wide as human psychology itself, such as timeliness, availability, ease of use, friendly and helpful service at the time of sale and afterward, personalization, and customization.

A key point in using this family of metrics is to *focus on specifications or expectations that are known and defined.* Consider, for example, a direct-mail computer company such as Dell or Gateway. Such organizations certainly have companywide aspirations regarding customer satisfaction. And many people at Dell or Gateway can use on-spec quality metrics to set and achieve goals that contribute to the whole company's customer satisfaction performance challenge. When a product is shipped, it should meet known specifications regarding the hardware and software to be included as well as whether that hardware and software work as promised. Moreover, both Dell and Gateway know that customers have specific expectations about the ease and speed of setting up their new equipment. Thus, goals regarding on-expec quality can also be set and monitored.

In contrast, customer expectations that are *unknown* cannot be *intentionally* achieved. You cannot set or achieve goals related to aspects of performance that you cannot even define. Should organizations ignore the unknown? Of course not. You can and should set goals to discover and meet new expectations that matter to customers. But these unknown aspects are better served through the family of metrics called *positive yields* (see below) than through on-spec/expec goals.

To succeed in the challenge of increasing the number of totally satisfied or delighted customers, organizations must deal with subjective issues such as feelings, attitudes, and emotions that cannot be fully captured through known specifications or expectations. Similarly, there are irreducible, abstract aspects to such overall aspirations as "most respected brand," "partnering relationships," and "total quality." Organizations should set and pursue such goals, using positive yields. But making unknown and elusive criteria the content of on-spec/expec goals only invites the same difficulty we saw with allocating CEO costs to purchasing. People will not have any useful way to problem-solve and seek improvements on that which remains unknown to them. By *including only what is known in on-spec/expec quality goals,* people can track and learn from failure. If, for example, Dell or Gateway finds that 40 percent of customer complaints concern the failure of a Microsoft program to boot up on the first try, a combined Dell or Gateway and Microsoft team can fix the problem. Of course, once the unknown becomes known, you can then easily include it in on-spec/expec goals.

In my experience, the most pragmatic on-spec/expec goals are expressed in terms of *not falling short.* That is, the goals seek to avoid the number and/or impact of defects, mistakes, or errors. For example, consider Motorola's Six Sigma aspirations. Six Sigma is a statistical measure that indicates less than four defects or errors per million opportunities for error. Motorola people enjoy telling audiences that, in comparison with Motorola's aspiration, most enterprises operate at between three and four sigma levels, that is, between 6,000 and 66,000 defects per million opportunities. By carefully and persistently setting Six Sigma goals, Motorola puts itself in a position to apply classic total quality tools to identify and overcome the root causes of defects.

Positive Yields

This last category is the catch-all yardstick. All the measures in this group reflect positive and constructive output or yield of organizational effort. These metrics answer the question, "What positive impacts are we trying to accomplish for our customers, for our shareholders, and for ourselves?" Many positive yields are familiar and objective: revenues, profits, number of customers, market share, new products, and the like. Others are not so familiar. The number of partnering, trust-based, or preferred relationships; the number of completely satisfied or delighted customers; the existence or strength of institutional skills or core competencies (e.g., flexibility or nimbleness); improvements in climate surrounding or morale among the people of the enterprise—these and other performance metrics provide ways to assess the positive yield of organizational effort.

Of the four yardsticks, positive yields are most prone to subjective and qualitative metrics, particularly for new kinds of performance challenges. When your performance challenge is to "build partnering relationships," for example, then setting a goal to increase the number or percentage of such relationships makes sense. But evaluating relationships is a subjective, qualitative matter. It is hard to reduce this performance aspiration entirely to objective, quantitative criteria. Please note, however, that subjective and qualitative goals are not bad or impermissible so long as they can be assessed and tracked with effective candor and honesty.

Notwithstanding such difficulties, positive yields often are the goals most directly related to the challenge at hand. Consider, for example, the aspiration to "build the most respected brand." As shown in Figure 2.5, many criteria provide leading (e.g., percent of viewers who accurately recall television or other advertising) or lagging (e.g., market share) indicators of having the most respected brand. The positive yield of brand respect remains, however, the most direct measure of respect. The problem is that brand respect involves any number of subjective and qualitative aspects, such as customer testimonials or survey results regarding brand preferences. So be it. As the saying goes, "You get what you measure." If your organization is serious about having the most respected brand, then you must work hard to understand and measure respect itself.

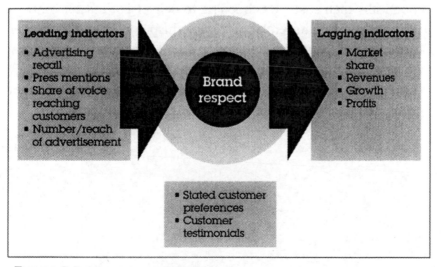

FIGURE 2.5 Most respected brand.

Good performance goals nearly always reflect a combination of two or more of the four yardsticks. Moreover, the first two of the four yardsticks (speed/time and cost) measure the effort or investment *put into* organizational action, while the second two (on-spec/expec quality and positive yields) measure benefits you *get out of* that effort and investment. *The best goals typically have at least one performance outcome related to the effort put in and at least one outcome related to the benefits produced by that effort.*

For example, a consumer products company seeking to increase the pace and impact of innovation might set a goal to *"reduce the time to market of new products by half while simultaneously doubling the hit rate of successful new products."* This performance goal reflects two of the four yardsticks: the speed/time of the new product development process (the effort put in) and the positive yield of successful new products (the effect of that effort). Were the organization to concentrate its effort solely on reducing the input to innovation (in terms of cost or speed/time), it would risk lowering the number of commercial successes. On the other hand, if the focus were entirely on the positive yield of new product successes, those new products might take a very long time to appear and might carry uneconomically high costs. By choosing to deliver *both* faster innovation *and* more commercial successes, the people at the consumer products company are challenging themselves to work creatively to solve the inherent tension involved in introducing more new products at a faster pace. (See Chapter 4 for further discussion of why and how to create "both/and" tension in your goals.)

Exercise 2.1: Losing Weight or Feeling Better?

Take a few minutes to write down whether you believe your performance challenges are more like "losing weight" or "feeling better," and the reasons for that conclusion. In particular, identify whether and to what extent any of the following difficulties exist regarding your performance challenges:

1. There is no universally recognized metric.

2. We must use at least some qualitative and subjective criteria (as opposed to only quantitative and objective metrics).

3. This challenge will require extra work and effort to monitor and measure.

4. We do not currently know our baseline performance.

5. We will need the cooperation of other people over whom we have no control or authority.

6. We do not understand the lead/lag relationship among the various metrics we might use to monitor performance.

7. The metrics with which we are most familiar are not specifically and directly relevant to this challenge.

8. It will be difficult for us to choose a set of metrics and stick with them long enough to learn and progress.

Make sure you discuss these observations with your colleagues and reach some common understanding about the obstacles you face.

Exercise 2.2: Brainstorming and Sequencing

This is a two-part exercise. First, take 20 to 30 minutes to brainstorm with your colleagues to create as complete a list as possible of the metrics you might use to monitor progress against your performance challenge. Remember to welcome suggestions of any metric that is *assessable,* no matter how subjective or qualitative it might be. Once you have your list of possible metrics, take the time to locate each metric in the sequencing chart that follows. This chart will help you identify leading and lagging relationships in your metrics. In the chart's first column, record those metrics that precede, lead, or cause the performance outcomes you are trying to accomplish. In the second column, record those metrics that directly and concurrently reflect the accomplishment of your performance challenge. Finally, use the third column for those metrics that lag or happen as a result of the accomplishment of your performance challenge.

SEQUENCING METRICS

Our performance challenge:

_____

_____

_____

Performance outcomes we seek:

_____

_____

Metrics that precede/lead	Concurrent metrics	Metrics that lag

Exercise 2.3: Choose Your Yardsticks

Consider the performance challenge and outcome(s) you have before you. Now brainstorm as complete a list of metrics as possible, using the four yardsticks:

Cost	Speed/time	On-spec/expec	Positive yields
____	____	____	____
____	____	____	____
____	____	____	____
____	____	____	____
____	____	____	____

Remember that today's performance challenges often demand more than purely financial and market metrics. Moreover, some of the best metrics might be subjective and qualitative as well as objective and quantitative. A metric is usable so long as you and your colleagues can assess progress toward a stated performance outcome. Once you have identified the list of possibilities from the four yardsticks, discuss among yourselves which make the most sense to use in rewriting your performance outcome(s). Then restate your outcome(s) or goal(s) accordingly.

CHAPTER 3

Get Specific

The SMART Cycle of Performance

Many of us have heard of the wisdom of working smarter, not harder. Working smarter starts with setting goals based on specific performance outcomes that matter. Isn't it nice, then, that so many people have discovered that the acronym SMART provides an effective guide to setting specific performance goals. Fewer of us, however, have learned that *achieving* performance goals requires committing ourselves to a *cycle of performance*—that is, to setting, pursuing, evaluating, achieving, and/or adjusting; setting, pursuing, evaluating, achieving, and/or adjusting; and so on (see Figure 3.1). Through the combination of these techniques, you and your colleagues can effectively learn how to deal with the difficulties inherent in so many of today's most pressing challenges.

Goals are SMART when they are:

- Specific: Specificity comes from answering such questions as "at what?," "for whom?," and "by how much?." It is not sufficient, for example, just to want to be the fastest. You

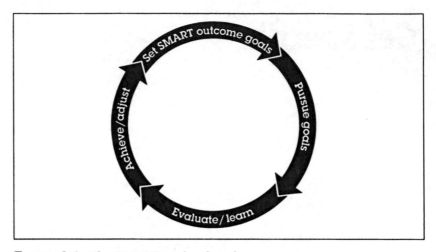

FIGURE 3.1 The SMART cycle of performance.

must define what you wish to be the fastest at. For example, you might wish to be the fastest at resolving customer questions. As Chapter 2 explained, once you have specified the process at which you wish to be fastest, you must further specify what you choose as the starting points and stopping points of that process. Similarly, it is not enough to seek to be the preferred provider or the company of choice. You must define which target customers, suppliers, employees, or other constituencies you hope will prefer you over all other providers. For example, people at a credit card company might seek to be the fastest at resolving customer questions for gold card holders. You also must specify "by how much." Consider, for example, the goal of "reducing the time to market of new products by half while simultaneously doubling the hit rate of successful new products." This goal uses number ("reduce by half" and "double") to tell us how much the company seeks to improve. Other numerical or statistical approaches include increasing, reducing, or holding constant such things as numbers, percentages, averages, ranges, minimums, and maximums.

- Measurable: Goals must be measurable, or at least assessable, if you and your colleagues hope to benefit from the tracking and learning so critical to performance. As Chapter 2 indicated, effective metrics might be either objective or subjective; what counts is their *assessability.* So long as reasonably candid and honest effort can evaluate progress, then even subjective goals are assessable. Naturally, the greater the ambiguity, abstractness, and subjectivity in the metrics, the greater the difficulty—approaching impossibility—of evaluation and assessment. You and your colleagues should use the four yardsticks introduced in Chapter 2 to identify and choose *measurable and assessable* goals.

- Aggressive yet Achievable: Both of these "A"s are significant. (Indeed, if you prefer, use the acronym SMAART as a reminder to seek goals that are both aggressive and achievable.) Aggressive goals provide the stretch that inspires us to aim and achieve higher than we might otherwise do. Still, most people do not pursue goals for very long if those goals are not credible—and credibility depends on some basic belief and confidence that we *can* achieve the goals we have set for ourselves. A manufacturing company that has not commercialized a fundamentally new technology in 40 years cannot credibly seek to introduce a dozen new products over the coming six months. But the same company can commit itself to introducing at least one new product successfully over the coming two years. *Most of us, in fact, can do at least one really new thing at least once over a reasonably short period of time.* Few of us believe we can do many really new things many times over a really short period. So, ask yourselves *how new* is this, *how often* must we do it, and *over what period of time.* Somewhere in the range of answers you will find goals that are aggressive yet achievable.

- Relevant: The goals you set should pertain directly to the performance challenge you confront. This sounds obvious enough. But when faced with new and different performance challenges, many of us have an unfortunate habit of picking goals based on lagging indicators such as revenues and profits that are not directly relevant to the challenge at hand. Or, worse, we use activity-based goals that only beg the question of how success is to be determined ("our goal is to plan how best to become innovative"). The most pertinent goals would neither lag nor lead—they would capture the exact performance outcomes we seek to achieve and do so concurrently with that achievement. For example, if Sears wishes to increase the number of customers who purchase from more than one department on each store visit, then a direct and concurrent metric is "multiple department purchases per customer per visit." Such directness is not always easy to achieve, but it is the best thing to try for. So, for example, when faced with a customer service challenge, you should choose goals directly relevant to customer service itself (e.g., *"We will cut the time to satisfied response in half, while simultaneously eliminating all errors in our response"*). And the same holds true for other challenges.

- Time-bound: It is not smart to pursue goals that are completely open-ended. You must answer the question: *By when?* Specifying the time frame for completion ensures that your goals are aggressive yet achievable. Remember the overweight, stressed-out friend from Chapter 2? When he said, "I'll lose 15 pounds," your first question was, "By when?" If he had replied, "Over the next few years," both of you would have laughed. Without the specificity of time frame, neither he nor you would know how serious his performance aspiration was.

  We know, then, that goals must be time-bound to be goals at all. However, the time frame selected should not automatically track the official organization calendar. Most of us have a tail-wagging-the-dog problem here. Deep habits derived from calendar-based financial and operations planning have left us thinking first about the organization's calendar and only second about the time frames inherent in of the performance challenges we face. Thus, we habitually ask, "What shall we do this year, or this quarter, or this month?" Instead, we should first ask what outcomes are best for us to achieve over what time frame. Only then should our goals be translated into a calendar if necessary for either internal or external communications and direction.

We must set goals *and achieve them*. Chapters 8 through 10 will examine a series of powerful management disciplines you can use to achieve the goals you set. At this point, it is important to emphasize that goal setting and goal achievement are intertwined. They form an *iterative cycle,* something you do over and over and over and over again. Figure 3.1 illustrates this SMART cycle of performance. To use it effectively, you and your colleagues should:

- *Set SMART outcome-based goals.* It may seem repetitious to continually emphasize this, but until you have set specific goals, you have not begun the cycle. Remember, there really are no perfectly right or best goals, particularly for today's most pressing performance challenges. Do the best you can, make choices, and get on with it. The power of the performance cycle arises from the setting, pursuing, evaluating, and resetting of goals. With time and effort, your goals will get better and better, smarter and smarter.

- *Exert at least the minimum effort required to progress and learn.* You and your colleagues (and everyone else) know that you cannot achieve performance goals without making some effort to do so. Goal achievement does not happen through incantations or fairy dust. You and others *know* when you are putting in *at least the minimal effort* needed to make progress. If you are, terrific. If not, have the courage to say so and stop the charade. Only when you have done enough work to be reflective can you begin to learn. This is as straightforward as asking, "*What worked?/What didn't?*," and then adjusting your approach.

■ *Use real time, not organization time.* There are two aspects of organization time that jeopardize the SMART cycle of performance. The first is organization calendar-based planning. As mentioned, don't fall into the trap of using habitual organization calendar time to set your goals. Rather, pick whatever aggressive yet achievable time frames make sense. Second, make certain that you and your colleagues *pursue your SMART goals between meetings,* that is, in real time. Yes, you need meetings to generate ideas, discuss and evaluate progress, and share lessons learned. But people who work on their goals only in meetings (in organization time) are likely to founder and fail.

■ *Iterate, iterate, iterate.* Treat the SMART cycle of performance as a cycle, not a one-time sequence of steps. Get to the second time through, then the third, and so on. As you do, you will be rewarded with mounting performance achievements; more interesting, challenging, and effective goals; new and powerful skills and capabilities; and an ever enlarging sense of excitement, enthusiasm, and accomplishment.

The following story illustrates the power of the SMART cycle of performance at work. Years of eroding enrollments had left a two-year language instruction program in jeopardy. Admissions officers privately pointed fingers at the quality of instruction. Instructors objected and openly complained that the admissions office was failing. As the school entered the admissions cycle for the new academic year, the head of the program asked a joint team of admissions officers and instructors to find a way to stem the erosion. Once the fireworks of mutual complaints had subsided, the team chose the following goal: "*We will grow applications by 30 percent and achieve at least some increase in the number of students attending in the coming academic year."* One more matriculating student than the previous year would have been enough; the team did not want to get more specific than that.

As team members worked together, they discovered many insights that might affect their results. Perhaps most significant, the admissions officers realized they had lost touch with some of the innovations and newer approaches the instructors were using. To capitalize on such insights, the instructors agreed to participate far more heavily in the admissions process than ever before. As a result, the instructors learned firsthand about the concerns and needs of potential applicants and students. The team worked hard to respond to those concerns as best they could in the current admissions cycle, but recognized that some improvements would have to wait for the next year's cycle.

When the due date for applications passed, the number of applicants had risen 32 percent over the previous year. The team and the program head were elated. Moreover, because team members had learned so much about prospective students, they now chose to adjust their matriculation goal to a specific increase of 10 more students than the preceding year. Again, they threw themselves into their work; again, they learned a lot. They found that prospective students depended heavily on word-of-mouth recommendations, particularly about customized instruction programs as well as getting through the first four to six weeks in the program.

That September, nine more students enrolled than had done so the year before. The team had fallen one student short of its goal, but remained so gratified about what they had learned and achieved that they told the program head they wanted to continue working together for yet another admissions cycle. They once again adjusted their SMART outcome-based goals. Now they sought *"to grow applicants by 25 percent and matriculants by*

15." Meanwhile, the team asked the program head to assemble another group of instructors, admissions officers, and students for the purpose of improving the way new students were integrated into the program upon arrival. They recommended that the program head give this new team a very specific charter: "*Figure out how to successfully integrate 100 percent of incoming students in no more than six weeks from the beginning of the academic year.*" This new team took its cue from the earlier team in pursuing the SMART cycle of performance and were quite successful. Eventually, several strategy, policy, and skill shifts emerged from the turnaround of this language program. At the core of this story, though, you find first one, then a second, team that set SMART goals, pursued and learned from them, evaluated progress, and then set newer and even SMARTer goals in a continuing effort to define and deliver the performance outcomes that mattered most.

Use Performance Trees to Convert Broad Aspirations into Specific Goals

Sometimes we begin the quest for performance with an aspiration so broad and so encompassing that we wonder how we can ever reduce the overall vision into SMART outcome-based goals that make sense. We want to "be the fastest," "be the best," "be the most customer-focused," "be the biggest," "be the best place to work," "be the most preferred." But we are not confident about the best set of goals to get us there. As we think creatively and enthusiastically about such challenges, we generate dozens of activities—things we might do to accomplish our aspirations.

Chapter 1 reassured you that such activities are important, but warned you against confusing these activities with outcomes. Chapter 2 provided you with tools and frameworks to select the most relevant metrics with which to monitor your success in pursuing any of these activities and the outcome-based goals that emerge from them. And this chapter encourages you to set SMART goals that can get you started on your iterative SMART cycle of performance. Now, I want to introduce you to a device that can help you convert expansive aspirations such as "be the best" into a series of specific, outcome-based performance goals that make sense.

Moving from comprehensive aspirations to specific outcomes demands that you focus or *dial in* on particulars. Imagine, by analogy, that you and your spouse are picnicking on a hillside overlooking a bay. The full beauty of the scene lies before you, and yet you cannot appreciate any details of its particular aspects without focusing. If you wish to appreciate the parts of the whole, you must select those parts and dial in. As you do, your understanding and appreciation of the scene grows. You discover much—objects, colors, juxtapositions, motion—that you had not seen before; so much, in fact, that you risk losing touch with the whole scene as your interest in the particulars grows. To avoid this, you find your eyes switching back and forth, from whole pattern to particulars and back to whole pattern, constantly learning more about what lies before you. And you do all of this collaboratively with your spouse, taking full advantage of each other's differing experiences and perspectives.

The challenge of moving from broad aspirations to specific outcomes is also a phenomenon of shifting between *pattern* and *particulars*. Consider the purpose of "being the most innovative." As you and your colleagues ponder what success would mean, you must develop both a whole vision or pattern of success as well as a variety of particulars. You can get better at breaking down such whole aspirations into particulars by using a device called a *performance tree.*

Figure 3.2 depicts a blank performance tree. Note that it is like a tree with trunk, limbs, and branches, but lying on its side instead of standing up. You fill in the blanks by moving from left to right, from aspiration to increasingly specific and detailed particulars. Thus, the trunk of the tree is the full aspiration itself (e.g., "to be the most innovative"); the limbs and branches represent the next two levels of increasing specificity.

A performance tree is nothing more than a three-part framework for logically breaking down a challenge into parts and, then, further disaggregating each part into subparts. These trees are equally helpful for very broad challenges ("to be the preferred provider") and very narrow ones ("Our sales team wishes to exceed all others in customer satisfaction"). Completing a performance tree is easiest if you do it in two phases. You should use phase one to make focusing choices about the objectives that are

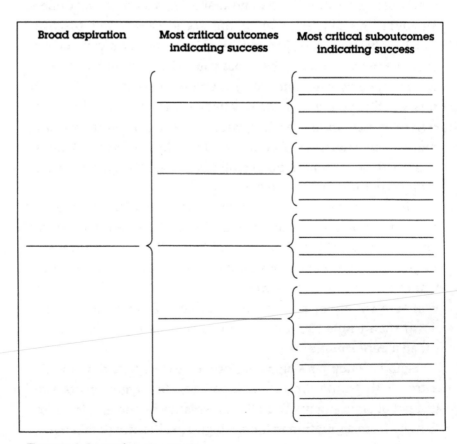

FIGURE 3.2 Performance tree.

most important. You should use phase two to convert those objectives into SMART outcome-based goals.

The following situation illustrates this. The leaders of the mainframe division (MFD) of a major computer company are sick and tired of being beaten up as the "dead-end division" by analysts, the press, customers, other company executives, and their own demoralized employees. They believe that if they can get out in front of the industry shift from client-server architecture to network computing, they can reinvigorate their business. They want to vastly improve their financial results, but they also earnestly seek to be the preferred place to work in their company as well as the preferred supplier among their customers. In their guts, they feel all of this has to do with being innovative. Accordingly, they choose to articulate their vision as: "Make MFD a place where new things happen profitably."

This leadership group is excited and inspired. They really can *see* the mountain they wish to climb. Now they turn to a performance tree to specify objectives and how to evaluate success. Using a performance tree involves the following steps.

Phase One: Specifying Objectives

- *Choose a time frame.* You must pick a specific time frame within which to focus your efforts. As discussed earlier, too many of us automatically assume we must pick the organization's annual calendar or strategic planning time horizon. But neither needs to be the case. Instead, you should pick what you believe is the most actionable time frame. The leaders of MFD decided to pick 6 to 15 months in order to avoid getting trapped into an orientation that was either too short-term or too long-term.

- *State your aspiration on the far left.* Put your vision, mission, aspiration, or chosen direction at the root of the performance tree on the far left. Be sure to include the time frame selected.

■ *With reference to your stated aspiration, ask yourselves, "What are the four to six most critical objectives we have to achieve to succeed?"* Choosing only four to six objectives ensures focus. Obviously, you and your colleagues should brainstorm as many candidates for action as possible. You will need to determine some logic and process for choosing among them. It is essential, however, that you make this choice. Without choice, there is no focus; without focus, there is no performance. (Remember that, as you and your colleagues succeed, the SMART cycle of performance will guide you toward expanding your initial choices, allowing you to add new choices that make sense.)

At the conclusion of a half-day's discussion, the leaders of MFD chose the following four objectives among dozens of possibilities: (1) making MFD the preferred division for employees of the company, (2) using network computing architecture as the basis for creating a "new things happening" image both internally and externally, (3) shifting significant R&D resources from maintaining established products to creating new ones, and (4) establishing new customers and channels. (See Figure 3.2, where, for space reasons, the "root" has been placed at the top instead of the far left.)

■ *For each of the four to six objectives selected, ask, "What are the three to five most critical things we must succeed at?"* Performance trees are designed to help you increase specificity and make choices. Thus, you must now identify the three to five most important steps or subobjectives necessary to success for each of the four to six critical objectives in respect to your overall challenge. For example, the leaders of MFD (again following extensive brainstorming and discussion) chose to focus on three things in order to succeed at using network computing architecture as the basis for creating a "new things happening" image both internally and externally: (1) Introduce successful new network com-

puting products, (2) gain recognition as experts in the field
of network computing, and (3) hold a network computing
technology fair that attracts substantial interest from the
press as well as potential customers not currently doing
business with MFD (see Figure 3.3).

Phase Two: Converting Objectives into SMART Outcome-Based Goals

■ *Convert the objectives in your performance tree to SMART outcome-based performance goals.* In phase one, you have

---

In the next 6 to 15 months, make MFD a place where new things happen profitably.

1 Make MFD the preferred division for employees.

    1.1 Improve employee satisfaction survey results.

    1.2 Improve employee communications.

    1.3 Provide employees with opportunities to make new things happen.

    1.4 Attract employees from other divisions.

2 Use network computing to create a "new things happening" image, internally and externally.

    2.1 Introduce new network computing products.

    2.2 Gain recognition as experts in network computing.

    2.3 Hold a network computing technology fair.

3 Shift R&D resources from maintaining established products to creating new ones.

    3.1 Reduce number of people who support old products.

    3.2 Obtain corporate investment in new product development.

    3.3 Introduce new network computing products.

4 Establish new customers and channels.

    4.1 Identify new, nontraditional sales channels.

    4.2 Identify and sell to new customers.

    4.3 Ensure that new channels and customer sales are profitable.

FIGURE 3.3 MFD's performance tree: phase one/objectives.

produced a rich picture of how to move forward with your overall aspiration. You have made critical focusing choices with respect to time frame and objectives. If you are like most people, and like the leaders of MFD in this example, you probably expressed those objectives in terms of activities (see Figure 3.3). Now you must translate these activities and objectives into SMART outcomes. For example, the MFD leaders chose two outcome-based goals with which to pursue success in gaining recognition as experts in the field of network computing: (1) *Receive at least three invitations over the next 15 months to deliver major addresses on network computing at major industry events,* and (2) *be cited for "new things happening in network computing" at least twice a month over the next year in prominent trade journals.*

Your task is to convert every item on the tree—root, limb, and branch—into SMART goal statements. Many people find it helpful to start either on the right side or the middle of the tree instead of the far left. Use the approaches, techniques, and exercises in Chapters 1, 2, and 3. For example, you should try to answer the question posed in Chapter 1, Exercise 1.2 ("How would you know success?") for each root, limb, and branch of your performance tree. As you practice, you will find it increasingly easy to convert phase one objectives and activities into phase two outcome-based goal statements.

■ *Review the emerging picture for completeness.* Brainstorming, discussion, deliberation, choices—this step-by-step introduction to performance trees has emphasized the kind of work you and your colleagues must do to take advantage of this powerful tool. After completing both phases, you must ask yourselves what, if anything, is missing? Have you forgotten anything? Have you placed too much emphasis on one or more aspects of the challenge? Could you select even better outcomes to pursue?

The first time the leaders of MFD went through both phases one and two, they ignored current customers. As a result, they decided to add a fifth limb to their performance tree, namely, "gain commitments to network computing from existing customers." They made choices respecting how best to accomplish this, and they converted both this new limb and its related branches into SMART outcomes that mattered.

Figure 3.4 presents the completed phase two tree in the case of MFD. Note that MFD's leaders converted most of the final tree into specific outcome-based goals, although some ("establish new customers and channels") remained activity-based. You may discover yourselves ending up with a mix like this, too. In the best case, you will convert the entire performance tree into SMART outcome-based goals. But if, like MFD, you end up with only 70 or 80 percent of the tree as outcomes, that's okay. Indeed, it will be far superior to having 100 percent activity-based goals. Compare the phase one tree of MFD in Figure 3.3 with the completed phase two tree in Figure 3.4, and you will see the power of a performance focus at work.

The purpose of performance trees is, first, to use logic to produce focus and choice (phase one), and then to use a performance orientation to convert objectives and activities into SMART outcome-based goals that matter (phase two). As you and your colleagues become experts at using performance trees, you will find yourselves combining both phases and increasingly articulating SMART outcome-based goals for the objectives you choose, without having to rely on activity-based statements at all.

In the next 6 to 15 months, make MFD a place where new things happen profitably.

1 Within 15 months, more than 70 percent of our people will consider MFD the preferred place to make a contribution.

   1.1 By December, identify and eliminate the five lowest-rated elements in our satisfaction survey.

   1.2 Reduce the cycle time to less than one week from the making of any major decision to the point at which all affected employees can articulate the performance outcomes they must achieve in pursuit of that decision.

   1.3 Redeploy at least 35 percent of employees from old products to new network computing products.

   1.4 Attract at least 15 high-profile, high-potential employees from other divisions within the next 9 months.

2 Use network computing to create a "new things happening" image, internally and externally.

   2.1 Introduce five new network computing products over the next 15 months.

   2.2 Receive at least two press mentions each month over the next 9 months regarding positive and new things happening in MFD.

   2.3 Receive at least three invitations to make addresses at major computer conferences this year.

   2.4 Hold a network computing technology fair in May that attracts at least 400 people, at least half of whom do not currently do business with MFD.

3 Shift 35 percent of total R&D resources from maintaining established products to creating new ones.

   3.1 Maintain current customer satisfaction levels regarding the support of old products, while simultaneously shifting at least 50 people into new product development.

   3.2 Gain at least $25 million of investment from the corporation for network computing technology.

   3.3 Introduce at least five new network computing products over the next 15 months that each achieve at least 10 percent penetration of existing customer accounts and purchases by at least 15 new customers.

4 Establish new customers and channels.

   4.1 Sell at least $10 million of private-label network computers through non-MFD resellers by next November.

   4.2 Gain network computer purchases from at least 15 customers in each of the following market segments by year end: banking, professional services, and retail.

   4.3 Achieve at least a 20 percent operating margin on all network computing sales in the current calendar year.

5 Gain commitments to upgrade from client-server to network computing from at least 20 percent of our existing customers.

   5.1 Achieve at least 10 percent penetration of existing customers with network computing sales over the next 15 months, while increasing customer satisfaction in those accounts.

   5.2 Gain firm commitments for network computing purchase within the next 24 months from at least an additional 10 percent of customers.

FIGURE 3.4 MFD's performance tree: phase two/SMART outcomes.

Using the exercises in Chapters 1 and 2, you and your colleagues have developed descriptions of the outcomes you hope to accomplish as well as the metrics you will use to monitor your progress. Now you can employ the following exercises to develop specific goals. It is best to do each of these exercises with the people who will contribute most to the achievement of the performance outcomes. Once again, several of these exercises overlap. Experience suggests, however, each provides a useful spin or angle on developing performance goals that matter. Use all of them until you are sure which ones work best for you and your colleagues.

Exercise 3.1: Dialing In—At What, for Whom, How Much, by When?

As you think about your performance challenge, ask yourselves to be as specific as possible about four key questions:

- *At what* are we trying to improve? This discussion might begin with a very broad concept such as "customer service." That's okay. But don't get stuck at such a general, high level. Instead, keep asking yourselves to dial in on the exact, specific thing you're trying to get better at. For example, perhaps you are trying to get better at "the timeliness and accuracy of responses to customer inquiries regarding products A, B, and C."

- *For whom* are we trying to improve at this? The best answer here is not, "Our boss." The most likely answer begins with customers (although it is not the only one—you might also be trying to get better at something for the people of the enterprise, for strategic partners, or for shareholders or other funders). Once again, you need to dial in. It is highly unlikely that you are trying to get better at something for all

WORKBOOK

customers. Instead, you probably need to focus your efforts on certain customers. To continue the customer service example, perhaps you are trying to get better at "the timeliness and accuracy of responses to inquiries regarding products A, B, and C from customers who have purchased goods from us at least five times in the past year."

- *How much* better are we trying to get? This is a simple question. But it requires that you have selected your yardsticks or metrics, that you have some sense of where you stand now in terms of performance, and, finally, that you pick a target and go for it. If you really do not know where you stand now, then pick a target anyway. For example, perhaps you do not know the current timeliness and accuracy with which you respond to inquiries from the target customer group. Instead of waiting to find out, go ahead and pick a goal and use your progress toward that goal to figure out where you stand. To continue the customer service example, your goal might be stated as follows: "to respond within 24 hours with zero defects to inquiries regarding products A, B, and C from customers who have purchased goods from us at least five times in the past year."

- *By when* will you achieve this goal? As you consider this question, recognize that the greater the number of people, departments, functions, and processes involved in meeting a goal, the longer it is likely to take. For this reason, if you and your colleagues are a senior management team setting a goal for your entire organization, then you can expect the completion date to *most likely* be several months in the future. Like all rules of thumb, this is not necessarily always true. On the other hand, if you are a frontline customer service team that regularly handles the kind of inquiries mentioned in the example, then the completion time frames should be quite short—for example, "no later than six weeks from now, to be responding within 24 hours with zero defects to inquiries regarding products A, B, and C from customers who have purchased goods from us at least five times in the past year."

Exercise 3.2: Get SMART!

If you have completed the exercises in Chapters 1 and 2, then you are in a very good position to use the SMART acronym as a guide. Ask yourselves, "Are our performance outcome(s) or goal(s):

	Yes, because:	No, because:
Specific?	_____	_____
Measurable?	_____	_____
Aggressive yet Achievable?	_____	_____
Relevant to our challenge?	_____	_____
Time-bound?	_____	_____

Exercise 3.3: The Schaffer Funnel

In his excellent book, *The Breakthrough Strategy* (Ballinger Publishing Co., 1988), Robert Schaffer exhorts people to begin change efforts with results. He also provides a powerful tool for articulating the kind of near-term, aggressive yet achievable goals that can help people start with results. I call this tool "the Schaffer Funnel." In effect, you ask yourselves how you can narrow down a challenge that seems big, long-term, and complex and requires effort from people far beyond your control or influence to one that is near-term, small, straightforward, and within your range of doability.

Here's an example:

From: Build sales through indirect channels to represent 40 percent of our total revenue.

> *To:* Identify and sign up distributors who can represent us on the West Coast and provide them with the needed product training.

> *To:* Select at least one distributor and cut a deal by December.

> *To:* Cut a deal with Consolidated Warehouses by December and gain at least $10 million of new revenues through them by February.

Pick a performance challenge and work your way down the Schaffer funnel.

Exercise 3.4: Good Goal Grammar

There is a grammar to well-stated performance outcomes and goals. Nearly always, such goal statements include the following:

- *Verb:* Examples are *increase, decrease, improve, deliver, grow, cut, expand.*

- *Object:* This tells people what you wish to get better at and for whom.

- *How much:* This typically includes both a target goal and a reference to the metrics of success.

- *By when:* This tells the time frame for completion of your goal.

You should check your goal statements against this good goal grammar and adjust them accordingly.

Exercise 3.5: Performance Trees

Construct a performance tree for your challenge. Remember to work through both phases of this exercise. In phase one:

1. Choose a time frame.

2. State your overall aspiration on the far left of the tree.

3. With reference to your stated aspiration, ask yourselves, "What are the four to six most critical objectives we have to achieve to succeed?"

4. Now, for each of these four to six objectives, ask, "What are the three to five most critical things we must succeed at?"

In phase two:

1. Convert the objectives in your performance tree to outcome-based, SMART performance goals.

2. Review the emerging picture for completeness.

CHAPTER 4

Beyond Stretch

Injecting Creative and
Personal Tension
into Goals

The Importance of Putting Our Hearts and Minds into Performance Goals

Most of us know about the benefits of stretch goals. We know we give our best in the face of difficult odds, particularly in organization settings. Indeed, as we discussed in Chapter 3, the "A" in SMART goals stands for "aggressive yet achievable." A strong performance orientation demands that we aim high. But we should take a moment to ask why. Why is it that people who aim high regularly outperform those who don't?

The answer lies in the *personal and creative tension* caused by stretch goals. When we take goals personally, we tap into who we really are. Pride, fear of failure, security, the good opinion of others, our basic sense of purpose, and aspirations—all these motivations powerfully shape our determination and focus. When we are personally committed to performance goals, when we put ourselves on the line for results, we are far more likely to give our very best. We want to succeed. We want to make a difference. We want to win. We put our *hearts* into our work.

Stretch goals have another potent aspect. When goals truly have stretch in them, we cannot be certain about achieving them. This causes us to pursue creative and risky approaches. We are far more likely to identify and try novel routes to problem solving, decision making, and implementation. We also are more likely to adopt a *learning stance* toward our challenge. Having taken creative risks, we ask what has worked, what has not, and why. We put our *minds* into our work.

In contrast, when our performance goals are both wholly familiar and routinely accomplished, we invest neither our full hearts nor our full minds in our work. The risk arises that we will become halfhearted nine-to-fivers who check our minds at the door. And, as so many of us have discovered over the past two decades of wrenching change, we also become targets for the next round of downsizing.

Because so much has changed in our organizations and the nature of the challenges that confront us, performance now demands more than ever before that we *tap into the power of goals filled with personal and creative tension.* All of us—at every level and in every part of every organization—must learn a variety of new skills, behaviors, and working relationships to continue making a difference to our organizations and ourselves. We know this. Yet, as I wrote about in *Taking Charge of Change* (Addison-Wesley, 1996), there is a harsh, unyielding truth at play here: *Only adults can take responsibility for their own behavior change.* No one else can do it for them.

Think again of your dieting friend from Chapter 2. Neither you nor any other person can take responsibility for changing the necessary behaviors (diet and exercise) of your friend. Only your friend can do that. Well, neither can you learn for me or for anyone else the team discipline, total quality and customer service skills and attitudes, how to reengineer, the relationship skills for effective strategic alliances, and other skills, behaviors, and working relationships demanded by today's most pressing performance challenges.

Each of us must take responsibility for our own change. However, more than 20 years of working with organizations and people facing change have convinced me of a profound, though subtle, reality: *Most adults most of the time are far more likely to take responsibility for their own behavior and skill change if they focus primarily on performance outcomes, not change.* Organizations across the globe are strewn with the wreckage of total quality, customer service, partnering, innovation, reengineering, teaming, core competency, benchmarking, and other strategic and visionary initiatives that asked people to commit to change instead of demanding that they commit to specific performance outcomes and goals that the change was supposed to facilitate. (See Chapter 10 for further discussion of this phenomenon that I call the challenge of behavior-driven change.)

If you and your colleagues wish to get yourselves and others to take responsibility for change, focus first and foremost on getting yourselves and others to make commitments to specific performance outcomes and goals that you believe will require the underlying change. For example, if you work at a bank and seek to make the credit process faster and more customer-friendly, don't ask yourselves to commit first to working in teams or collaborating across functions or listening to customers. Rather, gain commitments for outcomes such as "*reduce credit process time to less than 24 hours, while simultaneously requiring no more than 10 minutes of the customer's own time.*" The point is twofold. First, neither you nor your colleagues can achieve this performance goal without taking responsibility for learning a lot about teaming, collaboration, and customer listening. Second, experience suggests that you and your colleagues will actually learn more about teaming, collaboration, and customer listening by focusing on this specific goal than by committing only to learn the new skills alone.

Why is this? Why are you more likely to take responsibility for learning new skills, behaviors, and working relationships if you focus primarily on committing to performance outcomes and goals rather than committing to change itself? There are several reasons:

- *Basic organizational purpose:* Most people understand that the primary purpose and requirement of their organization is to perform and that their primary purpose is to contribute to that performance. Consequently, it makes sense to most people, when they are challenged, to commit to performance outcomes that matter to their organization. In contrast, most people noticeably hesitate when they are asked to commit to change for the sake of change. It is not that they don't buy into the notion that the change in question might be good. Who would argue against the value of collaboration, teamwork, or listening to customers? But when concrete, understandable connections between change and performance are left unspoken and unclear, most people remain convinced, and rightly so, that "this too shall pass."

- *Motivation:* In today's world, jobs are livelihoods in the fullest sense of the word. If your job is in an organization, then you associate that job with, and depend on it for, your most fundamental human needs for food, shelter, health and other insurance, affiliation and a sense of belonging, and, often, for a sense of purpose and meaning in your life. Changes that threaten your job stir up these motivations; they make you anxious about your future. Neither you nor anyone else can wholly eliminate such anxieties. You can, however, master them by finding a constructive focus for your energy and effort. The best focus is a *specific performance outcome that matters to the organization and your continuing participation in it*. In contrast, behavioral, relationship, and skill changes themselves are more elusive and harder to pin down. Just when and how, for example, can you or others be certain you have adequately learned how to team, or how to listen to customers, or how to have a trust-based relationship with a client? Consequently, if you set goals that are activity-based (e.g., "learn how to team in the next three months"), you will find it much more difficult to harness and master your anxieties.

- *Causality and adult learning:* For most of us most of the time, learning itself is a matter of observing cause and effect. The world of organizations is filled with the practical arts, with figuring out what works, what doesn't, and why. Identifying and connecting causes to effects, however, is notoriously complicated if the effects are primarily about relationships or behaviors or interpersonal skills (e.g., skills at interviewing, selling, teaming, and other things that we cannot do wholly by ourselves). We learn better when we can relate causes to effects that are specific, tangible, and assessable. For example, when we take a learning stance toward a performance goal such as "reduce credit process time to less than 24 hours, while simultaneously requiring no more than 10 minutes of the customer's own time," we are likely to figure out how to succeed. And, equally important, part of that success will depend on our taking responsibility for such skills and behaviors as teaming, collaborating, and listening to customers.

- *Outcomes versus activities:* As Chapter 1 discussed, when we pursue activity-based goals, we fall into the traps of unsustainability, demotivation, and confusion. It is worth noting that when we ask people to commit first and foremost to quality, customer service, reengineering, teams, strategic partnering, core competencies, boundarylessness, empowerment, innovation, and any other version of change, we are inviting—even encouraging—activity-based goals. The point is not that such underlying activities and changes are unimportant. They are urgent, important, and essential. But performance outcomes are the primary reason for such changes, not the changes themselves.

Many people will find these explanations critical, useful, and helpful. For others, it is perhaps more important to point to the hard facts of experience. So, let me say again: Repeatedly, over more than two decades, I have seen adult after adult, team after team, and organization after organization dramatically improve the odds that people will take responsibility for change if they first take responsibility for specific performance outcomes and goals. And the reverse is also, if unfortunately, true. When organizations as a whole, and the individuals within them, pursue change for the sake of change and activities for the sake of activities, they fail.

This, then, returns us to the lessons in stretch goals. If commitments to specific performance outcomes and goals are the road we must travel to master the highly personal and anxiety-filled challenge of change, then we must set and pursue goals that demand the very best we have in us. If we are to successfully master both performance and change, *we must put our hearts and our minds into our goals.* Stretch (the aggressive "A" in SMART) is one way to do so. It turns out that there are other important and relatively new ways to infuse our performance goals with the kind of personal and creative tension needed for success. Let's turn to them now.

Stretch and Beyond—Techniques for Putting Personal and Creative Tension into Performance Goals

As we've discussed, stretch goals demand that we put our hearts and our minds into the performance challenges we face. This section will introduce additional ways to ensure that you and your colleagues are fully invested in the goals you seek to achieve. First, we'll discuss how to infuse goals with the creative tension you need to master today's most pressing endeavors. Then, we'll turn to how you can use public approaches to setting and evaluating goals as a means to personalizing your efforts.

Creative Tension I: New Goals for New Challenges

"If you always do what you've always done, you'll always get what you've always got." Don't fall into this trap when you and your colleagues set performance goals. Instead, you can build constructive and creative tension by setting goals that directly measure success at today's newest performance challenges. In other words, construct new outcomes for new challenges.

Consider, for example, the need to be faster. Nearly every organization I know has accepted speed as a requirement for effective competition and customer satisfaction. Yet, if you look at the budgets and annual plans of most organizations, you will find performance goals stated entirely in terms of revenue, cost, margin, profit, head count, and various financial ratios. Hardly a word appears that relates to speed or time. This begs an obvious question: How can an organization get faster if it does not have "get faster" goals?

Does this mean that financial goals are bad or even completely irrelevant to becoming faster? No. Nor does it prevent such goals from having the characteristic of stretch. An organization might, for example, have a stretch goal in its plan "to reduce costs by 60 percent". That certainly has stretch in it! And, reaching such a goal will likely demand dramatically improved performance in terms of speed and time. Thus, the argument that a "get faster" aspiration should have "get faster" goals is not a condemnation or a suggestion that organizations abandon more traditional goals. It is an assertion that *the traditional goals, by themselves, are not enough*. They will not maximize the positive and constructive challenge and tension that you can and should seek to create.

Why? Well, there is a square peg, round hole problem here. People throughout the organization are discussing and debating the need to address the issues of time and speed, and then they look at the performance goals in budgets and plans and see nothing directly about time or speed in them. Two problems arise.

First, there is disbelief, even cynicism. When people see very aggressive goals such as "reduce costs by 60 percent" and they know they have been working for years to reduce costs, they may not find the goal credible. In contrast, when people see a new and unfamiliar goal such as "reduce time to market by 50 percent," they can think about the goal in fundamentally new and different ways and, therefore, are more likely to suspend their disbelief.

Second is the problem of habit. When we give people cost-cutting goals, they attack them in classic cost-cutting ways. They fall back on the tried and true. They use old ways to meet old goals. It is much more challenging and novel for people who need to "get faster" to have goals that are stated and measured in terms of "getting faster." Yes, people who have never been evaluated according to time or speed will be anxious about the change. However, when anxious people focus on specific, concrete goals (e.g., "resolve all customer questions within 24 hours"), most will harness their anxieties in a constructive way. Most will instill their efforts with *a creative tension directed at achieving—and learning how to achieve—new goals for new challenges.*

You and your colleagues can create constructive and positive tension by ensuring that you articulate and measure your goals in ways that directly reflect the new kinds of challenges you face. In the best case, you will identify one or more metrics that are *quantifiable, objective, and concurrently relevant* to the new performance challenge. Time and speed metrics meet these criteria for the challenge of "getting faster." At first blush, however, because challenges such as strategic alliances, core competencies, diversity, innovation, and self-directed work teams *are new,* you may question what, if any, effective metrics you can use. Indeed, as we discussed in Chapter 2, such challenges may not always be reducible to quantifiable and objective metrics. All the difficulties associated with the lack of a universally recognized metric, subjective and qualitative criteria, the need for extra work in measuring and evaluating, establishing the leading and lagging relationships among metrics, and, often, the requirement of participation by others can frustrate you in your search to set and achieve new goals for new challenges. Still, unless you make that effort, you will forfeit the chance to infuse your goals with the maximum amount of creative tension.

As you struggle with such difficulties, go back to Chapters 1 through 3 and use the exercises to focus on outcomes and get specific. In addition, the following can help.

Metrics and Goals That Are New to You May Not Be New to the World

For example, many critical challenges confronting government and nonprofit organizations grow out of a newly discovered necessity to generate sustainable economic performance in the face of shrinking resources and unprecedented competition. Consequently, such organizations are scrambling to build skills and competencies at general and financial management, integrated planning and budgeting, marketing, and sales, as well as cultures that respect instead of dismiss economic considerations. People in government and nonprofit organizations can and should borrow many metrics from the for-profit world, such as contribution margins, market share within defined target segments, and allocation of overhead approaches.

Meanwhile, organizations from all three sectors (government, nonprofit, for-profit) should scan for relevant experiences and approaches of others. For example, many Northern European organizations have worked hard for more than a decade to integrate environmental concerns into assessments of performance. North American organizations have spent just as long tackling diversity. Each could learn from the other. And, as mentioned, it has been several years since organizations around the globe first started tackling time-based competition. Some organizations (Motorola, for example) have made significant advances in using metrics related to speed and time. Another example is strategic alliances. Most major organizations have entered into one or more such relationships and have had enough experience to offer insights into how best to think about and measure the performance outcomes that matter.

Connecting Traditional Goals to Untraditional Methods or Approaches

Often, you and your colleagues can develop quantifiable, objective, and relevant metrics by marrying the familiar (e.g., revenues) to the unfamiliar (e.g., cross-disciplinary account management teams). I call these *hybrid* goals. These *hybrid* goals specify outcomes to be produced by activities; they marry outcomes to new activities. Consider the following hybrid goal: "*The five new account management teams will generate a 20 percent increase in revenues from their assigned accounts within nine months.*" In this example, revenues from particular accounts make the goal quantifiable and objective, while asking the new cross-disciplinary teams to generate those revenues makes the goal relevant to the new challenge. Note how different this goal is from a pure activity-based objective such as "form five new cross-disciplinary account teams."

Stretch is essential to hybrid goals. If the target is too easy (e.g., seeking a 1 percent increase in revenues instead of the 20 percent stated in the preceding example), the people involved will feel little need to try out new approaches. In cross-disciplinary account management, for example, there is almost always a reluctance on the part of salespeople to permit others on the team to have substantive, meaningful access to the client. Relatively easily achieved goals ("1 percent") will not require salespeople to overcome this reluctance because the goal can be achieved through familiar methods, approaches, and behaviors. On the other hand, stretch goals ("20 percent increase") that are married to unfamiliar, mold-breaking approaches are more likely to create the constructive and positive tension that can unfreeze the past and provide motivation and focus to create a new future. Figure 4.1 provides additional examples of hybrid goal statements.

Performance challenge	Example of hybrid goal
Customer service	In the next six weeks, use information gathered from customers to reduce the top two sources of complaints.
Strategic alliances	Develop three different combined service offerings and determine which produce the greatest increase in sales to current customers over the next four months.
Diversity	Ensure that at least 20 percent of our company's top performers represent the diverse population we seek to build.
Training	80 percent of individuals/teams we train will set and achieve performance outcomes by using the content we train them on.
Values/behaviors/best place to work	100 percent of leaders in good standing in our company will have achieved their last six months' promised performance outcomes the "right way."

FIGURE 4.1 Hybrid goals.

Using Strong Approximations or Indicators

There are times when the outcomes you and your colleagues seek to achieve stare you right in the face, yet are extremely difficult to measure. Consider, for example, the increasingly common aspiration to "delight our customers." The outcome here is obvious: delighted customers. Setting a performance goal such as "double the number of delighted customers over the next six months" is a good way to start. Still, it begs an obvious question: How will you know when a customer is delighted?

The short answer is that you can never know for certain if a customer is delighted. Even customers who say they are delighted are often reporting a feeling that can be notoriously short-lived. So, in order to set and achieve outcomes related to delighting customers, you must identify and pursue some set of strong, reliable indicators or approximations of delightedness. The good news is that this is not as difficult as it might seem. Consider, for example, the number of different products or services purchased by the same customer, how often and with what persistence the same customer repurchases, the volume of purchases by the same customer over time, business referrals by customers, customers who ask for more business without being prompted, and customer testimonials. These and other outcomes provide strong indicators of "delighted customers" that you can reliably use to achieve your overall goal.

Creative Tension II: The Art of "Both/And" Goals Instead of One-Dimensional Goals

For many of us, confronting today's most pressing performance and change challenges is like a high-wire act. We must get from an old world (the world of the "as is" or the "way we do things around here") to a new world (the world of the "to be" or "our new vision") without any precipitous falls. Think, then, of the image of a tightrope walker. As she traverses the challenge from the "as is" to the "to be," she must master the tension created by the clash between forces of gravity and those of forward motion. The tightrope walker succeeds by maintaining her balance between forces that are in a natural opposition to one another. Unduly favoring either one or the other causes failure.

You and your colleagues can learn from this image if you first take the time to consider the opposing forces inherent in your performance challenges and then create goals that explicitly address those forces. I refer to this as *setting multidimensional, "both/and" goals instead of unidimensional, "either/or" goals*. A classic sales force challenge illustrates what I mean. For decades, senior managers have struggled to get salespeople to pay attention to both revenue and profits. In what has become a ritualized response, salespeople contend that they should only be held accountable for either one or the other, but not both. Management, say the salespeople, can have greater revenue by lowering prices. Or management can have greater profits through higher prices if only management will set lower revenue targets. In a more subtle but recognizable variation of this, salespeople also argue that if management wishes to increase profit margins, then management should focus on getting some other group (some "they")—manufacturing, marketing, or other functions—to lower costs.

In today's world, this either/or, we/they approach is unacceptable. To get beyond it, executives, salespeople, and others must first recognize that revenue, pricing, and costs of sales are all in natural opposition to one another. Like the tightrope walker, the people of the organization must work together to balance these forces. They can increase their odds of success if they set performance goals that have a creative, "both/and" tension, such as "*In our 20 largest national accounts over the next nine months, we will increase revenues by 10 percent and profit margin by 12 percent, while holding prices constant.*"

A second familiar example comes from total quality. More than 20 years of experience with quality point to the irrefutable observation that the cost of quality is free; that is, when people succeed in applying total quality to their work, the cost of that work inevitably shrinks. In other words, it does not have to cost more money to improve quality. Nevertheless, people tackling quality for the first time predictably make an either/or assertion. They contend that you can have either increased quality (which will cost money and time), or you can have reduced costs that will jeopardize quality, but you cannot have both. Like the salespeople in the preceding example, this perspective comes from decades of working inside organizational silos and being challenged to deliver one-dimensional goals. In fact, when people collaborate across functions and departments, they easily rise to meet multidimensional, "both/and" quality goals such as "*Over the next four months, we will cut our costs of delivery in half, while simultaneously reducing errors from 3 in 100 to 3 in 1,000."*

"Both/and" goals have tremendous power because they demand creativity. Consider the following goal in an organization that has traditionally relied exclusively on direct sales to clients: "*Increase revenues from indirect channels by $10 million dollars, while simultaneously reducing our cost of sales by 20 percent.*" Remember that the cost of direct sales is typically higher than the cost of indirect sales. Yet, in organizations with strong historical dependence on direct sales, the temptation is to create only the appearance of an indirect sale, while continuing to have the direct sales force do most of the work. (For example, the direct sales force arranges to have a wholesaler or distributor record the sale, while the direct sales force itself provides most, if not all, of the sales support for that distributor's customers.) The "both/and" goal won't permit this. To achieve *both* the revenue gain *and* the reduction in the cost of sales, the sales force must rely on people in indirect channels to actually do most of the work related to selling. They have no other choice. By getting sales and marketing people to commit to this performance goal, the organization increases the probability that those people will take responsibility for learning how to collaborate with people in the indirect channel, as opposed to merely creating the impression of doing so.

Alternatively, consider the headquarters staff group that has been chartered to develop a new skill across the organization, such as quality, customer focus, teams, or continuous improvement. The classic inclination of such groups is to focus on activity-based goals such as the number of people trained within a given time frame. A far better test of their impact, however, comes from the actual performance outcomes achieved by those they train—for example, in the context of quality, the actual improvements in speed or customer service as well as reductions in time and cost. A "both/and" perspective can assist such staff groups tremendously. Consider the following goal: "*Over the next six months, we will have trained 50 teams in quality and 80 percent of them will have set and achieved quality goals that make a difference to our company's new market-driven strategy."* Staff groups pursuing a goal like this are more likely to creatively select the teams they train (e.g., those that can make an impact on the strategy); the timing of the training (e.g., after teams have set strategy-relevant goals); the design of the training (e.g., highly interactive and focused on the actual goals of the teams as opposed to abstract theory of quality alone), and the follow-up (e.g., persistent offers of further help to ensure that those trained do meet their goals).

Like anything new, it takes practice to learn how to set "both/and" goals instead of the more familiar, one-dimensional goals of the "either/or" variety. You can get started by recognizing a fundamental relationship always present in work—namely, the concept of return on effort or investment. You and your colleagues must ask yourselves what returns you are seeking (remembering to consider both nonfinancial and financial returns) and what level of effort or investment you seek to make (again, considering such nonfinancial indicators of investment as time or speed in addition to cost).

If you prefer a more homespun version of this, remember: You reap what you sow. In other words, you always seek to get something out of the work and effort you put in. Consequently, you can think about performance outcomes and results along two dimensions: (1) the effort you put in, the sowing, and (2) what you hope to reap from your effort. Familiar performance indicators of effort include cost, investment, time, head count, and machine/equipment/asset hours. Illustrations of unfamiliar "sowing" indicators include contracts bid upon, new product ideas pursued, new methods of production tried out, and number of probationary hires put through training. Familiar performance indicators of "reaping" include revenues, profits, market share, new accounts, and various on-spec/expec indicators of quality as measured by error or defect rates. Less familiar ones might include new contracts won, customer expectations met, and number of commercially successful new products.

There are always one or more creative "both/and" tensions between investment (sowing) and return (reaping). If you take the time to brainstorm lists of possible indicators in each area, you will find it easier to select specific performance dimensions in natural tension with one another. Thus, for example, recall the four yardsticks introduced in Chapter 3: The first two of these categories of metrics typically are about "sowing" (time/speed and cost); the second two are about "reaping" (on-spec/expec quality and positive yields). Effective "both/and" goals would always include at least one goal from the "sowing" category and one goal from the "reaping" category. It is important to recognize that these two dimensions would form a natural opposition to one another. Look at the quality goal: "*Over the next four months, we will cut our costs of delivery in half, while simultaneously reducing errors from 3 in 100 to 3 in 1,000.*" In this case, the "sowing" goal is to cut costs of delivery in half, and the "reaping" goal is to reduce errors (i.e., higher on-spec/expec quality). Doing both *simultaneously* requires people to *creatively* resolve the tension between these two goals. Figure 4.2 provides further illustrations of "both/and" goals for several of today's most critical challenges.

Personal Tension: Going Public

You and your colleagues can inject constructive *personal* tension into your goals by communicating them openly to other people who matter and by inviting those people to join you in evaluating progress. I call this *going public.* A well-known historical example of this happened when President John F. Kennedy committed to land a person on the moon within 10 years. The audaciously *public* nature of his announcement—proclaimed in the midst of the space race against the archrival Soviet Union—put not only Kennedy's *personal* reputation on the line, but also the reputation of the U.S. government, NASA, and even Americans themselves.

Performance challenge	"Both/and" goal example
Quality	Double the number of customer repurchases, while cutting total sales time in half.
Continuous improvement	In each of the next six months, identify and eliminate the top cause of complaints, while keeping total customer service costs constant.
Globalization	Over the next 18 months, increase nonhome market percent of total sales from 10 percent to 20 percent, while also growing home market sales at 25 percent per annum rate.
Brand	Over the next 15 months, triple the number of potential customers who say they prefer our brand without increasing advertising expenses at all.
Talent	Reduce the attrition rate of our high-potential managers from 12 percent to 8 percent, while also increasing their average tenure in current positions twofold.
eCommerce	Add 50,000 new customers in the next year, while also reducing our average new customer acquisition cost by 80 percent.
Reengineering	Provide at least 90 percent of freshmen and sophomores with all their first choice subjects without increasing total faculty head count or hours.

FIGURE 4.2 "Both/and" goals.

A similarly well-known example from the business world is General Electric's Work-Out process, in which people from various functions and departments gather for a multiday session that culminates with public commitments to achieve certain goals. In making such commitments in open forums, people at General Electric put their reputations and character at risk, which, in turn, creates a positive, personal tension for most of them. And when such personal tension is connected to concrete, specific performance outcomes instead of mere activity-based goals, GE people excel.

An important aspect of GE's Work-Out program is that the same people who make public goal commitments gather later to evaluate progress. Without this essential follow-up, the power of creating personal tension can evaporate. It is interesting that, as GE's experience with Work-Outs has grown, the company has invited suppliers and customers to join both the commitment and evaluation phases. As you can imagine, doing this puts even more personal tension in the goals of participants.

Many organizations have borrowed the Work-Out approach and customized it for their own challenges. Others have developed alternative, but similarly public, approaches to building motivational power behind goal commitments. Dun & Bradstreet, for example, honors teams that have made strides in quality at an annual Team Day. Motorola selects from among thousands of entrants in its annual recognition of people who have contributed to the Six Sigma goals of that company. Citibank regularly asks people to accept a Team Challenge to tackle a major issue confronting the bank and report on their accomplishments to the bank's senior executives. Other companies create web sites where people associated with quality or other performance initiatives are expected to register their goals as well as their progress. Many companies have Olympics or Chairperson's Awards of various stripes.

In yet another variation, organizations have announced the limited availability of resources or special opportunities obtainable only through an open and public application process. 3M has done this for seed money for new ideas. The state government of Minnesota did something similar to encourage new attitudes and approaches toward customer service. Siemens uses this method to build entrepreneurialism.

Each of these examples reflects companywide programs that encourage open, public goal commitments and evaluations. You and your colleagues, however, do not have to wait for your organization to formally begin such an initiative. You can go public right now. Doing so requires only that you identify relevant people who are affected by your performance contributions and that you invite those people to listen to your performance commitments and help you evaluate progress against the goals you set.

A moment's reflection and discussion quickly identify people to invite to your goal-setting and evaluation efforts: internal suppliers and customers and external suppliers and customers. So long as you and your colleagues keep this on a personal, informal level, you do not need permission. As you consider going public, remember that this is a suggestion that you open up your goal-setting and evaluation efforts to the scrutiny of others *just once*— just one time with respect to one aspiration. We are not talking about fundamentally altering the way your organization officially sets and evaluates the goals of everyone within the organization. That, surely, would require more orchestrated organizational action. We are only talking about you and your colleagues setting and achieving *one* "both/and" outcome-based goal, *one time* in the presence of people who truly benefit from and care about the achievement of that goal. *You can do this.* Thousands of executives, managers, and frontline workers have. And, having empowered themselves to do so once, most have figured out ways to do it again. So can you. You don't need permission. You only need a determination to perform and learn, learn and perform.

Exercise 4.1: So What's New?

This brainstorming exercise can help you and your colleagues better understand any new or different performance challenge. Start the exercise by agreeing on a description of your challenge. Now take 10 or 15 minutes to brainstorm as many reasons and explanations as possible for why each of you thinks this challenge is new. Basically, you are answering this question: What is new or different about this challenge?

Having generated as long a list as possible, spend time assigning each of your reasons or explanations to the following categories:

- We must benefit new or different stakeholders or constituencies.

- We must collaborate with new or different people within or beyond our company.

- We must apply new or different disciplines or approaches.

- We must assess progress using new or different metrics or yardsticks.

Now spend the necessary time to focus on the "so what?" of these insights. Specifically, try to agree on the most critical dimensions that are new or different or unfamiliar. Then use those dimensions as background for the exercises in this and other chapters.

Exercise 4.2: Hybrids

Spend time developing hybrid goal statements that marry outcomes with new approaches. As useful background, you might pay particular attention to Exercises 1.5 ("Scratching the Activity

Itch") and 1.7 ("Input—Output—Impact"), as well as Exercise 2.2 ("Brainstorming and Sequencing"). Complete the following steps:

1. Identify the outcomes you seek, in both traditional and untraditional terms.

2. Specify and define the new approach(es) to be used in achieving those outcomes.

3. Identify who is responsible for applying the new approach(es) to achieve the desired outcomes.

4. Articulate one or more hybrid goals by insisting that the desired outcomes be produced *only* by the application of the new approach(es).

Refer to Figure 4.1 for examples.

Exercise 4.3: The Tightrope Walker

Use the image of a tightrope walker to identify all performance outcomes or results that are in natural opposition to one another. Then ask yourselves which combinations would be the most difficult to achieve simultaneously, and why (for example, units sold versus price, defects versus time, defects versus cost, or high-quality partnering relationships versus cost of sales). With a complete picture before you, articulate at least three "both/and" goals that, if achieved, would significantly contribute to the performance challenges facing you and your colleagues.

Exercise 4.4: Better Goal Grammar

As indicated in Exercise 3.4, "Good Goal Grammar," well-stated goals have a verb ("increase"), object ("commercially successful new products"), amount ("twofold"), and time frame ("over the next 16 months"). *Better* goal grammar reflects the creative tension in "both/and" goals by including at least a second goal along with the first. For example: "*Increase commercially successful new products twofold over the next 16 months, while simultaneously*

WORKBOOK

cutting the time to market of new products in half." Challenge yourself and your colleagues to construct at least three "both/and" goals using better goal grammar.

Exercise 4.5: Throw a Performance Party

Identify people beyond your boss and departmental colleagues who are beneficiaries of your work. Such people might be internal or external customers as well as internal or external suppliers or partners. Think hard about the kind of performance outcomes that matter to such people. Then invite some of those people to join you in developing performance goals that could make a difference. Once your "performance party" is really going strong (i.e., you have several illustrations of powerful goals before you), choose a goal and commit to it. Ask those attending if they will help you monitor the process of going forward (or even achieving the goal), and then be sure to follow up at the appropriate times.

Exercise 4.6: Work-Out

Ask the appropriate people in your organization to design and conduct a Work-Out session aimed at generating and achieving performance commitments. The subject matter of the session should relate to some major initiative, and those invited should be in a position to contribute to the success of that initiative.

CHAPTER 5

Beyond Jobs

Pick Outcomes That Fit Your Working Arenas

From Jobs to Working Arenas

Forgive me. But I need to introduce you to a piece of language I call *working arenas*. Working arenas are where people make performance happen in organizations. They include—but go well beyond—your job. You certainly continue to make performance happen in your job. But you and a small number of colleagues also make performance happen in a team or on a project. You and people throughout your company contribute to the success of a major initiative (e.g., total quality or reengineering); initiatives are also working arenas. Your contribution matters to the performance of one or more cross-functional processes. Indeed, your efforts combine with those of all the people of your enterprise to ensure the performance of your whole organization—the largest, most encompassing working arena of all.

In the 1950s, we did not need the concept of working arenas because performance *always* happened in simple and self-explanatory places: jobs, departments, functions, and the business as a whole. If you had asked people in the 1950s how they or their organizations were performing, they would have told you about job performance, department performance, function performance, and business performance. Furthermore, in the orderly 1950s organization, these contributions all added up in a nice, tidy fashion. Individual job performances added up to department performance; department performances added up to function performance; function performances added up to business performance. Each of these four spheres of activity was actually a working arena, but, since the list was so small and so well understood, the concept of working arenas was not needed to explain them.

Nor was the concept of working arenas necessary in the 1970s, even though discussions of performance had expanded to include divisions, business units, corporate headquarters, and the corporation as a whole, in addition to jobs, departments, functions, and separate businesses. As we approach the end of the 1990s, however, the concept of working arenas is critical because the number, type, and time frames of arenas or opportunities within which people make performance happen have exploded. Today we not only perform in jobs, departments, functions, divisions, businesses, and corporate headquarters but also in special assignments, processes, task forces, initiatives, projects, teams, multibusiness groups, joint ventures, strategic alliances, communities of practice, centers of excellence, and more. In addition, we have any number of transitory performance opportunities that influence the customer's experience, including customer interactions ("moments of truth") that are physical (e.g., at the retail store), auditory (e.g., phone calls), in print (e.g., direct mail), and electronic (e.g., online sessions). As Figure 5.1 illustrates, the simple, static, 1950s world of organization performance has given way to a much more fluid reality.

"So what?," you might ask. Well, you cannot successfully set and achieve performance goals without accounting for this shift from job-department-function-business to the multiple working arenas of today's organizations. If you attempt to force-fit all of today's

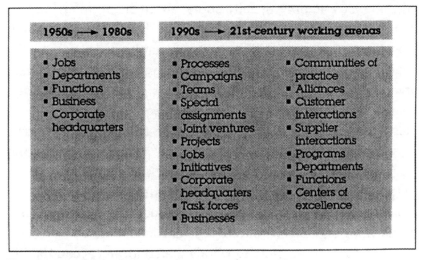

1950s ⟶ 1980s	1990s ⟶ 21st-century working arenas	
• Jobs • Departments • Functions • Business • Corporate headquarters	• Processes • Campaigns • Teams • Special assignments • Joint ventures • Projects • Jobs • Initiatives • Corporate headquarters • Task forces • Businesses	• Communities of practice • Alliances • Customer interactions • Supplier interactions • Programs • Departments • Functions • Centers of excellence

FIGURE 5.1 Where does performance happen?

necessary outcomes into an orderly job-department-function-business mold, you and your organization will fail. Instead, *you must identify the working arenas in which you contribute to any particular challenge and then shape SMART outcome-based goals to fit those working arenas.*

By the way, in introducing the concept of working arenas, the specific language itself is not the main focus. If you prefer other terms—such as *performance opportunities, performance arenas, contribution arenas, action arenas, contribution opportunities,* or *performance situations*—go ahead and use them. One company I know favored the concept of "global thought, local action" and used the term *local goals* to capture the idea of individual, team, project, initiative, customer interactions, and other working arenas. The key, then, is in the *meaning* behind the words *working arenas,* not in the words themselves. And that meaning is this: *You must set outcome-based goals that fit all the relevant working arenas, not just the jobs, of the people who must achieve those goals.*

This concept of *fit* is not new; you and your colleagues probably recognize it. Fit certainly applied to the well-ordered world of the 1950s. People usually speak about fit by referring to a time-honored managerial maxim that "formal accountability matches formal responsibility." When organizations operated like machines (job-department-function-business), this maxim made tremendous sense. If job performance led to department performance, which led to function performance, and, finally, to business performance, then it made sense to ensure that formal organizational accountability matched formal organizational responsibility. One could argue that for the greater part of the twentieth century, the formal scheme through which accountability matched responsibility was the bedrock on which well-performing organizations were designed and operated.

Today, it is impossible to wholly match formal accountability with formal responsibility. Performance challenges overlap too much and change too often. Consider an organization that embraces quality. The most successful quality efforts derive from a belief that the customer defines quality. In terms of the four yardsticks in Chapter 2, you might choose metrics for quality that include speed from the customer viewpoint, on-expec outcomes from the customer viewpoint, and various positive yields, again from the customer viewpoint. Could you put quality goals into everyone's formal job description? Yes. But doing so would not be enough. You could not completely match the performance challenge at hand with job-by-job, department-by-department, and function-by-function accountabilities. Inevitably, many critical outcome-based goals of quality require that teams and/or individuals contribute to business processes that cut across formal job-department-function boundaries. Trying to fit such outcomes into formal job-department-function descriptions would fail.

This does not mean that organizations cannot use the maxim that accountability matches responsibility to achieve some rough approximation of how the work and responsibilities of an organization are divided up. But I am arguing that a rough approximation is the best that's possible in today's fast-moving world. I am also exhorting organizations to avoid wasting time and resources in a hopeless attempt to apply the 1950s version of fit to twenty-first-century realities. Down that path lie the endless reorganizations that produce inaction and frustration.

Instead, you and your colleagues should apply a new version of fit. And that returns us to working arenas. Accountability for outcome-based goals must *fit the working arenas* of those people who will achieve the goals. As Figure 5.1 shows, there are both *formal* working arenas indicated by the organization chart (such as jobs and functions) and *informal* working arenas not found on that chart (teams, projects, initiatives, processes, electronic sessions with customers, etc.). Fit still makes sense. Our task now is to apply it to both the formal and the informal working arenas relevant to the success of any given challenge.

With this in mind, let's look at a major quality initiative in a Fortune 500 company. The initiative is 15 months old. Here are examples of some of the many formal and informal working arenas in which people are trying to make quality happen in this company:

- Quality action teams seeking near-term improvements in speed, customer satisfaction, error reduction, cost reduction, and/or revenue enhancements. Sometimes these quality action teams correspond to formal departments; sometimes they cut across formal departmental boundaries.

- Individuals seeking specific improvements in their interactions with internal and external customers. All of these efforts could be written into the formal job descriptions and goals of the individuals in question.

- Process reengineering initiatives seeking dramatic improvements in speed and error reduction in major cross-functional work flow processes. None of these efforts match up with the formal organization chart.

- Leadership teams of the process reengineering initiatives that are overseeing these initiatives. In this organization, none of these leadership teams have ever been held accountable for process outcomes.

■ Teams that are contributing to particular aspects of the process reengineering initiatives. For the most part, these contributing teams cut across formal department boundaries.

■ The quality initiative leadership team guiding the overall quality initiative. This team has become a part of the formal organization; its outcome-based goals can be written into the team's formal statement of accountability.

■ The head of quality guiding the overall initiative. She has a new, formal job in the organization and her formal accountability should match her formal responsibility.

■ Certified quality initiative trainers who conduct training and other support efforts. At this company, these trainers have other jobs. Through certification, they gain the organization's permission and encouragement to provide training and support to others on a part-time basis. As such, training is an informal job.

■ Certified quality initiative consultants who work with leadership and other teams in helping to integrate quality into the organization. Again, these internal consultants have other jobs, but through certification they take on additional challenges of providing help in the quality initiative.

■ Senior business leaders who, as individuals and as leadership teams, try to "walk the talk" and otherwise show support and leadership for the quality effort. Formal goals related to quality have been written into the individual job descriptions of these leaders. Their *team* accountabilities for leading quality, however, remain informal.

The blend of formal and informal shows itself strongly here. While the head of quality, the quality initiative leadership team,

individuals seeking to better satisfy internal and external customers, and senior business leaders operate in working arenas
that are part of the formal organization, the rest of the people
described here are making contributions informally. Asking any
committee to try to force-fit all the quality goals into formal individual, departmental, and functional accountabilities would be a
waste of precious time. While that committee labored, no
progress would be made toward reducing errors, increasing
speed, satisfying customers better, reducing costs, building skills
of people, growing revenues, or anything else.

This point is critical. Imagine the wastefulness of trying to
force-fit performance expectations into the machine-like, formal
job-department-function-business mold. Indeed, many of you
have probably experienced such wastefulness, whether in the
context of quality or some other major initiative. If so, you have
watched and waited while some group has fought and debated
over the best way to align the formal organization against a fast-
moving challenge heavily laden with cross-functional and cross-
organizational boundary realities. And while you have waited,
any number of performance opportunities to learn new skills and
behaviors to better serve customers and generate better returns
to shareholders have gone unattended.

The challenge today, then, is not to fit performance goals and
outcomes to the job-department-function-business mold. Rather,
it is to ensure that outcome-based performance goals fit the *working arenas* in which those goals must be achieved. Doing so, of
course, demands that you become familiar and comfortable with
defining the working arenas that make sense for the challenges
you face, which is the topic of the next section.

Fitting Goals to Working Arenas

The first four chapters of this book have concentrated on helping
you shape SMART outcome-based goals to meet today's most
pressing performance challenges. Organizations, however, rarely

achieve performance without first disaggregating, or breaking up, the work required and then asking people to set and achieve goals for that work. The concept of working arenas can help you divide up work in ways that include but go beyond the formal job-department-function-business model. It frees you to ask a critical series of six questions, each of which makes it easier to apply the tools and techniques of Chapters 1 through 4, including:

- **What is the performance challenge at hand?**
- **What outcomes would indicate success at this challenge?**
- **What are the working arenas relevant to this challenge?**
- **To which of those working arenas do I (or we) contribute?**
- **What metrics make the most sense for these working arenas?**
- **What SMART outcome-based goals should we set and pursue for each of these working arenas?**

Consider the challenge of building and maintaining the best brand. If I were to ask you the most basic question from Chapter 1, "How would you know you succeeded at building the best brand?," your answer might point to outcomes regarding brand respect and loyalty from customers as well as results for shareholders. If I then asked, "How would you go about achieving these outcomes?," you would describe the myriad working arenas in which best brands are created and maintained, including the coordinated advertising and promotion efforts to establish customer promises, as well as the work needed to create, sell, deliver, and service products. You also would include a variety of customer interactions and experiences that determine the effectiveness with which your company's promises to customers are fulfilled.

In effect, you would break up into subparts the overall challenge of building the best brand. Those subparts are working arenas. And, if your organization hopes to succeed at building the best brand, then each relevant working arena must set and achieve SMART outcome-based goals that make sense. As Figure 5.2 illus-

Working arena	Category of working arena	Outcome-based goals
Customer interface	Moments of customer interaction	Reduce customer time to access our products via electronic or telephonic means to no more than 15 seconds.
Advertising	Function	In the next advertising campaign, double the number of target customers who instantly recall our two central promises of "most convenient" and "lowest price."
Distribution	Function	Make our entire product line available within no more than three miles from every target customer's residence.
Order generation through delivery process	Process	Cut our average cost of sales and delivery in half and use the cost savings to maintain at least 10 percent lower price than lowest-priced competitor.
Quality	Initiative	Ensure that at least three out of four quality action teams set and achieve outcomes that increase customer convenience at the same or lower costs.
Whole business	Business	Increase the number of new customers by 50 percent and double the number of customer repurchases over the next 18 months through broadening the number of access points and reducing customer access time, while also increasing profit margins 10 percent.

FIGURE 5.2 Becoming the best brand.

trates, achieving success at becoming the best brand demands outcomes from a variety of different working arenas.

Let's use the quality effort we have been exploring in this chapter to further illustrate how you can use the abovementioned questions to gain clarity and specificity in your goals. This company has more than 50,000 people who work in over 40 countries around the world, delivering products and services to millions of customers. Like most Fortune 500 companies, this one competes in dozens of different businesses. The CEO has decided to use quality to deliver better value to customers, enhance shareholder returns, and provide skills, opportunities, and rewards for the people of the enterprise. The CEO answers the question, "What is the performance challenge at hand?," as follows: "Everyone in this company must use the tools, techniques, and philosophy of quality to significantly enhance customer value from the customer's point of view." In response to the question, "What outcomes would indicate success at this challenge?," he wants "A companywide fivefold increase in speed and fivefold reduction in errors over the next 18 months."

Given the complexity of this company's businesses and markets, it won't surprise you that there are many types of working arenas relevant to the quality challenge. For each separate business in each geographic market, the following working arenas exist:

- Specific moments of customer interactions, including:

    Prepurchase information and sales

    Purchase

    Use of product or service

    Help with product or service

    Payment

    Help with complaints

- Functional and cross-functional work that supports these moments of customer interactions, including:

Functional work such as marketing, sales, research and development, manufacturing, operations, billing and accounts receivable, and customer service

Cross-functional work processes such as order generation through fulfillment, integrated logistics, new product and service introduction, and customer service

- Management processes that support decision making about direction and resource allocation to support the work processes that support the customer interactions, including:

Strategic and operational planning, budgeting, and review

Communication

Hiring, deployment, and development of people

Technology innovation, upgrading, and maintenance

Reward, recognition, and career paths

In addition, the quality initiative itself has several working arenas, including the work of the head of the quality initiative, the leadership team guiding the quality initiative, the quality training and support sessions and interactions, and quality consultant sessions and interactions.

Armed with a list like this, people can answer the question, "Which working arenas do I (or we) contribute to?" Here are examples of how some people at this company responded.

- A customer service representative in Indonesia is focused on improving quality in two working arenas. The first is part of his job, namely, answering customer inquiries about products, taking orders, and updating customers on the status of their orders—all over the phone. He is also contributing to a second arena as a member of a cross-functional team redesigning the entire work flow process from customer inquiry through delivery of product.

■ The head of this company's French subsidiary contributes—both as an individual and as the leader of the top
management team—to a number of working arenas involving management processes such as (1) integrating quality
performance expectations and reviews into strategic and
operational planning, budgeting, and review; (2) communicating the purpose and results expected from quality, and
how those outcomes integrate with the overall direction of
the business; and (3) ensuring that quality performance
outcomes are included in reward, recognition, and career
development schemes. In addition, this business head is a
member of a cross-functional team redesigning the work
flow process by which customers receive financing assistance with major purchases.

■ A software engineer at headquarters contributes directly to
a number of new product development projects. In addition, she is on a cross-functional team developing new
approaches to obtaining customer input into the new product development process. Finally, she has been certified as a
quality trainer and, twice a year, leads training sessions for
people in different parts of the company. These training sessions are also working arenas.

■ A human resources executive at the company's Latin Amer-
ica regional headquarters is working with a team of line
managers and other human resource professionals to
redesign the process by which executive-level candidates
are hired and integrated into the company.

As you read through these illustrations, note the following patterns. First, most people contribute to only two or three working
arenas related to quality at any one time. Second, all of their contributions come either as individuals or as members of teams.
Third, only when people understand their working arenas can
they convert the abstract challenge of "using quality to enhance

customer value" into specific, outcome-based performance goals that fit and make sense.

Once people have identified a specific working arena, they can answer the question: What metrics make the most sense? Indeed, as we saw in the fivefold goal mentioned earlier, the CEO has embraced speed and defects from the customer's point of view as the metrics for the largest working arena of all: the whole company. With each of their respective working arenas in mind, the people we have just described asked:

- Who is the customer of this working arena?
- What is the first and last step of the work or process to be timed?
- What would the customer consider as defects?

For example, the Indonesian customer service representative is a member of a team redesigning the process from customer inquiry through delivery of product. Team members have identified the customer as those Indonesians who are in the market for the products in question. They have also defined the first and last steps of the work flow process as "first customer inquiry through first use of the product by the customer." Finally, they have begun a systematic effort to speak with customers and to comb through company service and complaint files to catalog defects from the customer point of view. Having done all this, the team set an aggressive and specific outcome-based performance goal: "*Ten weeks from now, for all new customers, we will have successfully cut the time of our process in half, while simultaneously eliminating all known defects.*"

The team recognizes that this goal is only the start of its overall mission to redesign the customer inquiry through delivery process. Team members know, for example, that they have chosen to focus first on new customers and on known defects. Such choices make this team an excellent example of using performance to drive change. Instead of directing its energy at plans and activities, the team is focused on outcomes. With early success and learning, the team will move on to set other, more encompassing goals by using the SMART cycle of performance described in Chapter 3.

This team's working arena is the process from first contact through first use. And the team's goal of cutting process time in half while simultaneously eliminating all known defects *fits* that working arena. The team's accountability matches its responsibility. However, the same goal would not fit the job of the Indonesian customer service representative. The responsibilities associated with his job are too narrow to encompass the full process here. Indeed, if he were assigned sole accountability for this goal of cutting process time in half while simultaneously eliminating all known defects, he would complain about a *violation* of the maxim of fitting responsibility to authority!

To sum up, through identifying relevant working arenas, you can characterize the *work* needed to accomplish any given performance challenge. By knowing the working arena in question— that is, the work that needs to be done—you can identify how you and others contribute to that work and the metrics and goals that indicate success at that work. Thus, to pick another example from this company's quality initiative, the software engineer is part of a team trying to figure out how best to integrate customer input into the product development process. The work involved includes developing new products and gaining customer input. The team will judge its success by evaluating the impact of customer input on the overall speed and defects of the new product development process.

The Problem of Indirect Working Arenas

As people at this company developed outcome-based goals to fit their working arenas related to the quality effort, a critical pattern emerged: *the distinction between direct and indirect performance contributions.* And this pattern shed light on the important, but sometimes hazardous, concept of the *internal customer.* Let me explain.

Those individuals and teams contributing to working arenas having direct contact with external customers found it easier to answer the question, "Who is the customer?," than did those people who contributed to working arenas that only indirectly influenced external customer value. In the examples from the previous section, each of the following working arenas contributed *directly* to value received by external customers:

- The telephone sessions of the Indonesian customer service representative
- The Indonesian customer inquiry through delivery process
- The financing process in France
- The customer input sessions related to the new product development process

Conversely, the various managerial support processes in France, the quality training sessions conducted by the software engineer, and the executive talent recruiting process did not involve working arenas with direct customer contact. Instead, the customers (i.e., users) of these working arenas were internal.

The good news regarding an internal customer orientation is that it permits people to answer the three critical questions about customer identity, first and last step of process, and defects from the customer's point of view. Thus, the team reworking the executive talent hiring and integrating process was able to use these questions to determine that its customers were men and women being considered for positions and that defects were anything these people—both as candidates and as new hires—considered as negatives in the hiring and integration process.

Perhaps most interesting was how this team determined the first and last steps in its process. Team members debated between designating the first step as the point when an executive-level position came open versus that point when any potential candidate first expressed interest in working for the company. There were good arguments on both sides. But, in the end, they decided on the latter because of the dictate to take the customer's point of view. (Note that if the team had defined the *customer* as the executives looking to hire new people, as opposed to the new people being hired, then arguably the first step in the process would be the point at which a job opening occurred.) They also chose to define *integration* as that point when a new hire could satisfactorily articulate the direction and goals of the company, the direction and goals of the new hire's part of the company, and how the new hire's own specific goals contributed to each. With all of this, the team was able to formulate the following goal: "*By September, we will eliminate all defects related to new hire misconceptions about purpose, direction, goals, and role, while simultaneously reducing the average time from expression of interest through integration to three months.*"

The hazards of the internal customer orientation arise when people making indirect performance contributions lose sight of the external customer and generate activity-based goals. Consider the quality training sessions at this company. The sessions themselves involved no direct contact with customers. Instead, users for the training sessions were internal people at the company seeking to learn how to use the philosophy and tools of total quality. Consider, then, the goal-setting challenge facing the software engineer. The tendency is for people in her position to set activity-based goals regarding the number of sessions conducted, the number of people who attend, and the satisfaction of those attending. Such goals have all the deficiencies we discussed in Chapter 1. No one can really answer, "How would you know these sessions made any difference that mattered?"

So what to do? I have found that people in indirect working arenas can succeed by using the hybrid activity/outcome-based goals discussed in Chapter 4. To do so, *first identify the direct contributions your internal customers make to their external cus-*

tomers. Enabling your internal customers to improve their direct impact on performance is the paramount reason for your work. Accordingly, your outcome-based goals should track the pattern illustrated in Figure 5.3.

For example, this software engineer asked herself, "What are the quality outcomes that matter to the external customers of those people attending my quality training sessions?" This helped her to shape the following goal: "*Three out of four people attending my quality sessions will, either individually or in teams, set and achieve speed and defect goals that matter to their customers within 10 weeks after the completion of the session.*" Note that this is a hybrid goal: It marries outcomes in speed and defect reduction to activities related to training.

If you and your colleagues work in an indirect working arena, ask yourselves:

- Who are the internal customers for our working arena?

- In what working arenas do these internal customers *directly* influence the outcomes that matter to the overall performance challenge in question?

- How can we formulate a goal that will marry our work to the performance outcomes we hope these internal customers will contribute?

The ultimate test of any activity is performance. As illustrated by the quality initiative recounted in this chapter, however, not all working arenas directly influence the ultimate outcomes sought. The various managerial support processes of concern to the

Nature of your work with internal customers	→ *that leads to* →	Specific outcomes produced by your internal customers for their external customers

FIGURE 5.3 Indirect arenas/hybrid goals.

French country head, for example, only indirectly contribute to increased speed and reduced defects for external customers. Consequently, it is more difficult for the country head here—and for anyone (including you) who might be involved in an indirect working arena—to set goals that matter. By using the questions listed above, you can identify the ultimate outcomes that matter most and use the technique of hybrid activity/outcome goals to drive success.

WORKBOOK

Exercise 5.1: Identifying Your Working Arenas

Take some time, either alone or in a group, to identify all the various working arenas to which you make a contribution. You should approach this exercise from a number of perspectives, including:

- *Organization chart:* Look at the organization chart and identify the formal working arenas to which you make a contribution, including your job, your department, your function, and your business.

- *Performance challenges:* Make a list of the most critical performance challenges facing your company. With respect to each challenge, use Figure 5.1 as a guide to identify as many working arenas as possible. Star or highlight the working arenas to which you make a contribution.

- *My assignments/tasks:* Make a list of all the assignments and tasks you currently have. As you look over this list, use Figure 5.1 to identify the working arenas that are relevant to your assignments and tasks.

Exercise 5.2: Match Metrics to Arenas

Once you have identified all of your working arenas, go back to Exercise 2.3 ("Choose Your Yardsticks"). Match the yardsticks or metrics that you believe make the most sense to each of your working arenas and performance challenges.

Exercise 5.3: Direct versus Indirect Working Arenas

Take the list of working arenas you generated in Exercise 5.1, and, with respect to each arena, identify whether your work contributes directly to customers, directly to results for shareholders, or directly to outcomes that matter to the people of the enterprise. If the answer to any of these questions is no, then identify the internal customers for your arenas. Ask and answer the following questions:

- Who are my internal customers?

- Do my internal customers contribute directly to outcomes that matter to customers? To shareholders? To people of the enterprise?

- If yes, how do my internal customers make a difference?

- How can I/we make a difference to the way they make a difference?

Use the information generated to articulate one or more hybrid goals for your indirect working arenas.

Exercise 5.4: SMART Outcome-Based Goals That Fit

Use the exercises in Chapters 1 through 4 to craft SMART outcome-based goals that fit your working arenas. Make sure that each outcome is relevant to the particular performance challenge at hand and is consistent with the scope of the work done in the working arena in question.

CHAPTER 6

Coordinate Your Goals with the Goals of Others

Apply Logic to Goal Alignment

Let's turn our attention to the challenge of alignment and coordination. Organizations are not organized if people in them pursue divergent, conflicting, and unrelated goals. In the spirit of innovation, organizations can tolerate, even encourage, some degree of misalignment. But not outright conflict and contradiction. There is no organization in the world with unlimited resources and opportunities (not even Microsoft!). Consequently, organizations must focus scarce resources and attention on their most important opportunities and challenges. By coordinating goals, organizations ensure focus because everyone works together to achieve the same overall objective.

No one really argues with this. The question is how to achieve coordination and alignment in a world filled with complex, overlapping, and fast-moving performance challenges, most of which demand more than financial outcomes for success. To answer this, we need to look hard at our managerial habits, especially those inherited from an era when financial performance *was* all that mattered. Let's review the job-department-function-business organizational model so deeply imprinted in our minds, a model reinforced by the pyramid view of organizations (see Figure 6.1). Think about the following propositions that so many of us take as the gospel on how organizations always have worked and always will work:

■ The *only* performance that matters is financial; it is *the* bottom line.

■ Optimal financial performance depends on an effective division of labor (because people get better and better at doing the same thing over and over again).

■ Labor should be divided to best match the natural talents and potential of people with the different jobs required to produce financial performance. Accordingly, we divide labor as follows:

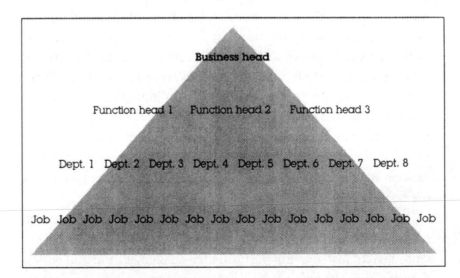

FIGURE 6.1 The pyramid model is the deepest assumption and belief about how organizations work.

Some people are inclined toward making and/or delivering products or services; we'll put them in operations.

Some people are inclined toward selling; we'll put them in sales.

Some people are inclined toward conceptualizing, communicating, and pricing products or services; we'll put them in marketing.

Some people are inclined toward leadership; we'll put them in management.

■ Financial performance is the *arithmetic* result (the bottom line) of the revenues generated by the efforts of sales and marketing minus the total cost of operations, sales, marketing, and management.

Simple, right? Well, most people *intellectually* recognize that this view of organization performance is incomplete for the chaotic world of the 1990s careening into the twenty-first century. These assumptions, however, were not off the mark for most of the twentieth century. They worked. They, and the pyramid model they fostered, explained the performance of most organizations and most economies for the past century. Consequently, they shaped our most fundamental managerial practices about how to set and align goals through annual budgeting and planning.

Here's how alignment happens according to the pyramid and its related assumptions (you will recognize this). Once a year, senior management guides the organization in the development of the annual budget and plan. Their objective is to build a complete picture of how the organization will produce the best possible financial performance for the coming year. They ask people in marketing to conceptualize, communicate, and price the projected volume of products and services that will generate the most revenues. They also ask marketing people to control their costs. They ask people in operations to set goals to deliver the volume targets projected by marketing at the lowest possible operations cost. They ask salespeople to meet the volume and revenue targets based on the prices and volume projections of marketing. They ask salespeople to control their costs.

The annual budget and plan presents a total picture of financial performance that translates into specific goals for every function, department, and job. The head of operations, for example, knows what volume must be delivered and, therefore, how best to set specific volume and cost goals for each department in operations. Each department head, in turn, knows how to translate departmental goals into individual job goals. The head of sales is in the same situation. He or she can translate total sales goals into region or territory goals; region or territory heads can translate those into individual salesperson goals.

Moreover, all the individual, departmental, and functional goals throughout the organization are in alignment. People in operations know what they must do and how their goals relate to the goals of their colleagues in marketing and sales, and vice versa. Everyone understands how their individual, departmental, and functional goals matter to the whole organization's bottom line. And the explanation for all of this—for how everyone sees the alignment of job, department, function, and company goals—is that it all adds up. *Literally* adds up.

Alignment and coordination in the pyramid model, then, derive entirely from the simple mathematics of traditional business. As illustrated in Figure 6.2, everyone sees how their goals align with each other and with those of the organization because they understand their role in this traditional formula for success. This inherited view of alignment and coordination has heavily shaped our deep traditional views of how organizations work (the pyramid model) as well as the simple mathematics of a formula for success that indeed adds up.

Enter chaos. Enter globalization; deregulation; reregulation; information and communications technology; new, multiple, and competing distribution channels; demographic shifts; and abundant and open capital markets. Enter competitive advan-

(Volume × Price) – Cost = Profit		
Marketing	Set volume and price	Watch costs
Sales	Deliver volume at set price	Watch costs
Operations	Deliver volume	Watch costs
Management	Ensure all the above	Watch costs

FIGURE 6.2 The traditional formula for success in business.

tages dependent on delivering the highest, most customized value to each customer at the lowest possible cost and the fastest possible speed. Enter competitive advantage grounded in core competencies and skills instead of geographic barriers or government licenses. Enter success that turns on people and brand—on intangibles not easily represented in financial terms. Enter a world of organization performance that includes but clearly goes beyond financial dimensions alone.

As Chapters 1 through 5 discussed, this new world of organization performance includes outcomes and metrics about speed, customer-defined defects, satisfaction of customers and people of the enterprise, and quality of relationships with partners, alliances, and clients, in addition to cost, revenue, volume, head count, and market share. And this new world of organization performance demands alignment of goals for working arenas that stretch well beyond the pyramid model of job-department-function-business. Today, then, we have a serious problem. Classic approaches to alignment, such as annual planning and budgeting, fall short. New metrics, new goals, and new working arenas don't match our deeply embedded beliefs about how organizations work. Nor do they conveniently add up in the arithmetic manner of revenues and costs. With these new difficulties come new dilemmas for coordination and alignment.

Let's say your organization seeks to compete on the basis of speed by being "the fastest." The annual plan sets overall company objectives to optimize financial performance and to be the fastest. Now it comes time to subdivide these overall goals into subgoals that can be assigned and coordinated throughout the organization. We know what happens to the revenue and cost goals: They are set, assigned, and coordinated according to the pyramid model and practices just discussed. But what happens to the speed goals?

Organizations have learned that asking each individual jobholder to become faster is not the way for the *organization as a whole* to become faster. Rather, overall organization speed depends far more on improving the speed of processes that cut across jobs, departments, and functions than on increasing the speed of task completion within jobs, departments, and functions. Accordingly, in pursuit of your company's objective to be the fastest, management will assemble cross-functional teams to speed up a series of critical *processes,* such as new product development, order generation through fulfillment, and customer service. Assume this happens. And assume that each of the teams working on these processes sets SMART outcome-based goals that use speed as the key metric of success.

The questions arise: How do these time-based goals align and coordinate with one another? How do they all add up? The answer is that, while you can take the steps we will discuss in the Mindbook section that follows to align such goals, you cannot make them add up. As Figure 6.3 illustrates, you cannot add up speed the way you can add up revenue, cost, or profit.

Why not? The answer lies in mathematics. Note that the revenues of product or business X add up with those of Y and Z because the unit of measurement—dollars—has the identical meaning across all three. A dollar is a dollar is a dollar. The dollar is truly a common denominator of performance across X, Y, and Z product or business lines. In contrast, the units of time that measure speed in Figure 6.3 do not reduce to a common denominator for the processes listed. If you literally added the four average speeds in Figure 6.3, you would get 6 months, 40 days, and 5 min-

What are the total revenues of ABC Company?		How fast is ABC Company?	
Product/business line	Revenues ($ millions)	Core process	Cycle time to completion
X	$30	Order generation through fulfillment	15 days
Y	$15	Customer service	5 minutes
Z	$45	New product introduction	6 months
Total	$90	Billing through collection	25 days
		Total	?

FIGURE 6.3 The limits of arithmetic.

utes. Yet answering the question, "How fast is ABC Company?" with the answer, "6 months, 40 days, and 5 minutes," makes no sense.

Arithmetic fails when you are trying to work across the *different processes* listed in Figure 6.3. However, arithmetic does not fail when working *within* any one of these processes. Thus, for example, consider the order-generation through fulfillment process at ABC Company. According to Figure 6.3, the average speed of this process is 15 days. Imagine that a series of teams contributing to each step in this process currently performs as follows:

- Receipt of order teams: 2 days
- Operations and logistics teams: 10 days
- Receipt of deliver teams: 3 days

Because these teams contribute to the speed of the *same* process, their times do add up. For the teams contributing to order generation through fulfillment, a day is a day is a day. A day is a *meaningful* common denominator. If goals were set for each of these teams to subtract a day from its current performance, then the order-generation through fulfillment speed would go from 15 days to 12 days. *Quantitative* alignment works inside the same process but fails to work across different processes.

This failure in using arithmetic does not condemn the organization to misalignment. Rather, when it comes to the challenge of improving organizational speed, *you align and coordinate goals through the common sense of qualitative logic instead of the arithmetic of quantitative logic.* Look again at the cycle times in Figure 6.3. As the people working in cross-functional teams strive to speed up each process, they can readily see how their efforts point toward making ABC Company as a whole faster and, most important, they can discuss and determine among themselves how and when their respective efforts either logically reinforce one another or don't. For example, the team working on order generation through fulfillment must avoid shortcuts that could slow down the customer service process. While arithmetic is not at work here, common sense is. And it is common sense grounded in *logic.*

Interestingly, arithmetic itself is a type of logical relationship. Let me expand on this a bit because if you see this point, you will have far less trouble aligning and coordinating today's most challenging goals. The arithmetic relationship among revenue and cost goals is *one kind* of logical relationship, a *quantitative* one. For example, when people in operations work on meeting their production volume and cost goals, common sense and logic tell them they are in alignment with those in marketing and sales who are striving to meet arithmetically similar volume, revenue, and cost goals. The logic of arithmetic, then, makes the organization's goals aligned.

Viewed this way, we can see that coordination and alignment have always demanded a *logically reinforcing set of goals* throughout the organization. It is just that, for the better part of the twentieth century, our managerial habits focused on one particular type of logic, namely the *quantitative* logic of arithmetic. Today, we must also use *qualitative* logic when needed. As indicated in Figure 6.4, we can and should continue to use the quan-

Today's performance challenges	Quantitative alignment	Qualitative alignment
Core competencies		✓
Customer service	✓*	✓
Diversity	✓*	✓
Electronic commerce	✓	
Growth	✓	
Innovation	✓*	✓
Mergers/acquisitions	✓	✓
Profitability	✓	
Reengineering	✓*	✓
Relationship-based marketing		✓
Speed	✓*	✓
Strategy	✓	
Teams		✓
Technology	✓*	
Total quality	✓*	✓
Values/behaviors/best place to work		✓

*Use arithmetic to align goals that have a meaningful common denominator.

FIGURE 6.4 Quantitative and qualitative logical alignment.

titative logic of arithmetic for financial challenges. We should also use arithmetic to align goals for nonfinancial challenges *within the limits of finding a meaningful common denominator* (as explained in the speed example of Figure 6.3). But when arithmetic fails, we must embrace qualitative logic to ensure alignment of goals that do not add up.

Use Arena Mapping to Break out of the Pyramid

Armed with both qualitative and quantitative logic, you are ready to take the next step toward coordinating goals: breaking out of the pyramid. The pyramid view of organization is like a suit of clothes. When organization performance is measured solely in financial terms, the suit fits very well. But when organization performance demands nonfinancial outcomes, the pyramid is a straightjacket. You and your colleagues can use *arena mapping* to free yourselves from the insanity of trying to force-fit nonfinancial challenges into the financially driven pyramid view of organization. In arena mapping, you map goals across the working arenas that make the most sense for any particular performance challenge (see Chapter 5), and then you apply quantitative and qualitative logic to ensure that these goals reinforce one another.

To illustrate arena mapping, let's first consider the case of a single business (we'll discuss multibusiness corporations later). Instead of visualizing this single business as a pyramid, consider the picture presented in Figure 6.5. In it, the business's working

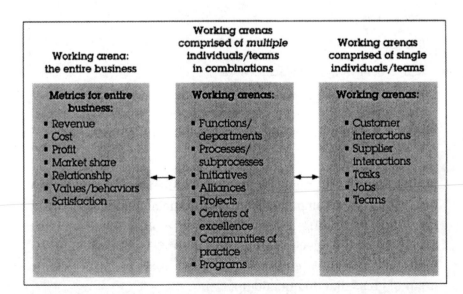

FIGURE 6.5 Arena mapping in a single business.

arenas are sorted into three groups. The largest, most encompassing working arena is on the left; it represents the entire business. The middle box captures the next largest set of working arenas: functions, cross-functional processes, special projects, and initiatives. Note that each of these arenas comprises work done by multiple individuals and/or multiple teams in combination with one another. Moreover, the performance outcomes of arenas in the middle box contribute to the overall performance of the entire business (i.e., the leftmost box). Finally, the far right box contains those working arenas—moments of customer interactions, project teams, and so on—that contribute to arenas in the middle box. Note that all of the work in these working arenas is done by single individuals or single teams.

Look for a moment at the double-headed arrows between the boxes. These arrows symbolically pose the central question of alignment: *Do the outcome-based goals of the various working arenas inside each box logically reinforce the working arena goals inside the adjacent box?* Arena mapping forces you to ask whether single individuals and/or single teams in the rightmost box have set goals that logically reinforce the goals of functions, processes, and/or initiatives in the middle box and, in turn, whether these functional, process, and/or initiative goals reinforce the overall goals of the whole business in the leftmost box. Arena mapping helps you:

1. Subdivide the work needed to achieve any performance challenge into the working arenas that make the most sense.

2. Specify SMART outcome-based goals for those working arenas.

3. Apply quantitative and qualitative logic to ensure that those goals are in alignment.

Arena mapping permits you to break out of the pyramid. Unlike the pyramid, which *always* portrays organization performance as the sum of functional, departmental, and individual jobs (Figure 6.1), arena mapping gives you a far more flexible tool for how best to view the *work and goals* needed to meet any particular performance challenge. If a challenge is best accomplished through work done in functions, departments, and individual jobs, then terrific—arena mapping allows you to approach the challenge in that manner. But if, as in the cases of speed, reengineering, or total quality, the performance challenge is best met through organizing work in processes and teams, then arena mapping provides you with the framework to ensure that work goals are aligned.

Let's return, then, to the example of your company seeking to be the fastest in addition to optimizing financial performance. Imagine that a number of cross-functional teams have been chartered to reengineer three critical processes (e.g., new product development, order generation through fulfillment, and customer service) under the overall guidance of a Reengineering Coordinating Team. In addition, your CEO asks people throughout the organization to form "Speed Now" teams for the purpose of immediately improving time-based performance. There is a Speed Now Coordinating Team overseeing the Speed Now initiative. Finally, the CEO in her wisdom, has made it clear that she does not want to pursue speed at the risk of deterioration in customer satisfaction. Speed Now efforts must deliver both speed and customer-perceived quality.

Remember that your organization is also pursuing optimal financial performance through an annual budget that subdivides financial goals into function, department, and individual goals. So your company has two broad performance challenges: speed and financial performance. Figure 6.6 shows the arena mapping for each of these challenges, and you can see that the working arenas and metrics required to meet the financial challenge differ from those required to meet the speed challenge. Thus, *arena mapping helps you view the work of your organization in whatever way makes the most sense to meet the particular performance challenge at hand.*

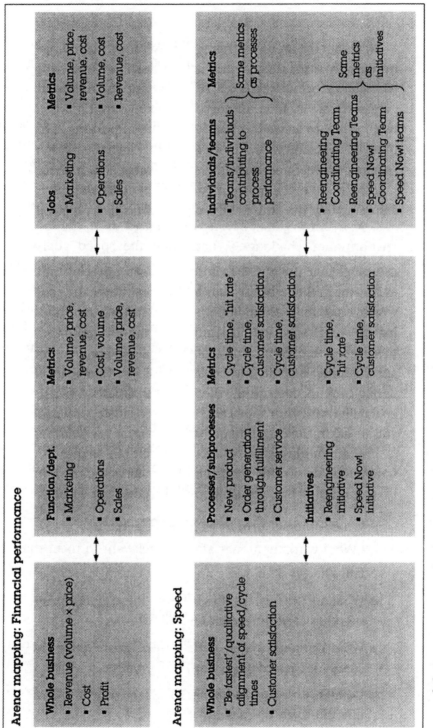

FIGURE 6.6   Arena mapping for financial performance and speed.

Note that the arena mapping for the financial challenge in Figure 6.6 only turns the pyramid on its side. If you rotate Figure 6.6 90 degrees clockwise, you will see the pyramid. Thus, arena mapping permits you to continue to use the pyramid model of work when it makes sense to do so. But, more important, it also permits you to *see* the work of your organization in the different ways required to meet new and different performance challenges.

Are the financial goals of your company in alignment? Well, assuming that the annual budget and plan specify goals that add up, yes, your organization is well aligned to meet the financial performance challenge. What about the speed goals? Again, assuming that the SMART outcome-based goals of individuals and teams in the rightmost box logically reinforce the goals of the working arenas in the middle box, and those of the middle box logically reinforce the organization's aspiration to be the fastest, then, yes, your organization is also well aligned to meet the speed and customer satisfaction challenge. (If you find yourself wondering how to determine whether your financial performance goals align with your speed and customer satisfaction goals, then you are asking an excellent question. Chapter 7 will address this.)

Arena mapping gives you the flexibility to align and coordinate the goals of *any* performance challenge confronting your organization. To use arena mapping effectively, you must answer:

- What is the performance challenge at hand?

- What working arenas are most relevant to meet that challenge?

- What are the best metrics to use in these working arenas for this kind of performance challenge?

- What outcome-based performance goals make the most sense for each of these working arenas?

- Do all of these goals logically reinforce one another, either quantitatively or qualitatively?

Arena mapping does not require you to *formally* restructure and reorganize to meet every different performance challenge your organization faces. (Chapter 9 will discuss questions of organization design relevant to organization performance.) However, arena mapping does obligate you to identify the working arenas that make the most sense for any given challenge and then set and align SMART outcome-based goals for those working arenas. As you gain comfort and experience with arena mapping, patterns will emerge, particularly respecting the distinction among initiatives, functions, and processes in the middle box and between individuals and teams in the rightmost box. For example, speed, quality, customer service, and reengineering challenges almost always involve processes in the middle box supported by teams in the rightmost box. Conversely, as we have seen, classic financial challenges often demand functional performance in the middle box and individual contributions in the rightmost box.

Let's now move from the case of a single business to organizations with many unrelated businesses (multibusiness corporations). As shown in Figure 6.7, arena mapping requires the

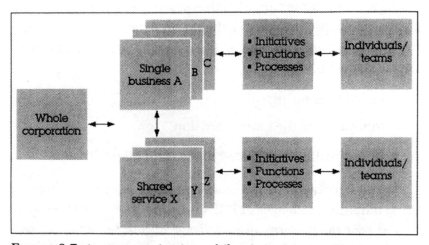

FIGURE 6.7 Arena mapping in multibusiness corporations.

addition of two more kinds of working arenas: the whole corporation and shared service units. Shared service units contain working arenas delivering services used by two or more of the corporation's businesses. These might be classic functions such as human resources, finance, and legal as well as shared resources such as manufacturing, distribution, and research and development.

As you look at Figure 6.7, the arrows once again pose the essential issue of alignment: Do the outcome-based goals of individuals and teams logically reinforce the goals of relevant initiatives, functions, and/or processes? Do those initiative, function, and process outcomes logically reinforce the performance goals of businesses and/or shared service units? Do the outcomes for shared service units and businesses logically reinforce one another? And, finally, do the goals of businesses and shared service units reinforce the goals and aspirations of the whole corporation?

To illustrate this, let's consider RBP Company, a multibusiness corporation that has three businesses: razor blades, batteries, and pens. In RBP Company, information technology, human resources, finance, and logistics are shared services. Figure 6.8 shows working arenas in RBP Company that *might* be relevant to any particular performance challenge. To determine which working arenas *are* relevant, look at the following performance challenges facing RBP Company:

- Reengineering logistics

- Innovation in the battery division

- New distribution alliances in the razor blade division

Figure 6.9 illustrates the working arenas relevant to each of these different challenges at RBP Company. *The important point here is that the performance challenge at hand determines how best to view the work of the organization and, therefore, how to*

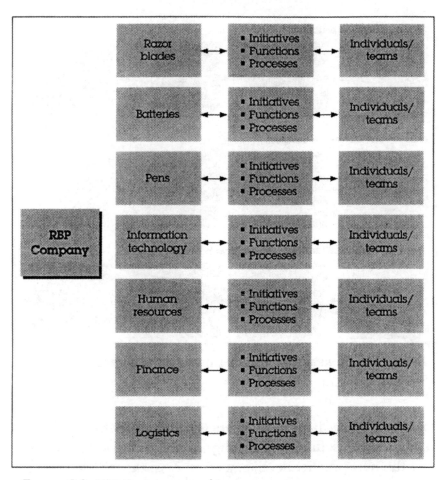

FIGURE 6.8 RBP Company working arenas.

set and coordinate goals. Note that each of the three arena mappings in Figure 6.9 presents a much simpler view of RBP Company than that shown in Figure 6.8. Multibusiness corporations are very complex entities. By taking a performance-driven approach, however, you can simplify the problem of setting and coordinating goals for any particular challenge. Thus, for example, the innovation challenge for the battery business does not demand that goals be set and coordinated in every one of the

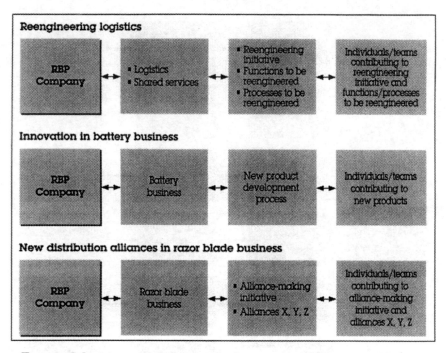

FIGURE 6.9 Arena mapping for performance challenges at RBP Company.

working arenas depicted in Figure 6.8. Rather, the primary focus should be on setting and aligning SMART outcome-based goals for the new product development process, the individuals and teams contributing to that process, and the specific new products going through it.

Exercise 6.1: Finding the Limits of Arithmetic Alignment

Make a list of all the performance challenges and initiatives currently on your organization's agenda. Use Exercise 2.3 ("Choose Your Yardsticks") to identify the metrics that make the most sense for each of these challenges and initiatives. Now discuss among yourselves the limits of arithmetic, if any, with respect to each challenge or initiative. Determine when you have a truly meaningful common denominator and when you don't. Decide when you must rely on qualitative logic instead of arithmetic to make sure that goals are coordinated across the organization. (Refer to Figure 6.4 as a guide.)

Exercise 6.2: Arena Mapping

Pick a performance challenge or initiative that matters to the success of your organization. Using Figure 6.5 as a thought starter, spend time identifying the most important working arenas in which this challenge will be met. Which of these arenas reflect the efforts of single individuals or single teams? Which arenas represent the work of combinations of multiple individuals and/or multiple teams? How do the arenas you have selected array themselves across the three boxes? (Or, if you are in a multibusiness situation, across the full set of boxes shown in Figure 6.7?)

Exercise 6.3: Arena Mapping, Metrics, and Alignment

Consider the arena mapping you and your colleagues have constructed in Exercise 6.2. Now, with the performance challenge in mind, select the metrics that you believe make the most sense for measuring success in each of the working arenas you have identified. Once you have completed this, look at the whole mapping and determine among yourselves the extent to which you must use qualitative and quantitative logic to align goals.

WORKBOOK

Exercise 6.4: Arena Mapping and SMART Outcomes

Using the arena mapping and metrics you produced in Exercise 6.3, construct a set of SMART outcome-based goals for each of the critical working arenas identified. This exercise might take several hours. The key is to use whichever exercises from Chapters 1 through 5 will help you identify specific goals for each of the key working arenas. Once you have done this, look at the whole picture and ask yourselves whether you have succeeded in aligning and coordinating goals throughout your organization for the performance challenge in question.

CHAPTER 7

Integrate Financial and Nonfinancial Goals

MIND BOOK

Understanding Cause-and-Effect Relationships among Goals

You can use the tools and techniques of the first six chapters to set and coordinate the outcome-based goals required to succeed at any given performance challenge facing your organization. But what about coordinating the goals of *different* performance challenges? And how do you make sure the goals throughout your company make sense in terms of customers, shareholders, people of the enterprise, and other key stakeholders? Moreover, how can you be certain that your short-term goals reinforce the goals that will take longer to achieve? Fully integrated goals, then, must address a variety of dimensions: different working arenas, different performance challenges, different stakeholders, and, different time frames.

Let's turn to the task of coordinating goals across different performance challenges. Most organizations today must master most of the following challenges in order to succeed:

- Alliances
- Core competencies
- Customer service
- Diversity
- Electronic commerce
- Growth
- Innovation
- Mergers/acquisitions
- Profitability
- Reengineering
- Relationship-based marketing
- Speed
- Strategy
- Teams
- Technology
- Total quality
- Values/behaviors/best place to work

Success starts with using the tools and techniques of Chapters 1 through 6 to set and coordinate SMART outcome-based goals for each separate challenge. In addition, however, total organization performance requires that the goals make sense *across* the challenges. That, in turn, depends on *understanding the leading and lagging relationships among the various performance challenges in question.* Or, if you prefer, it starts with identifying the *cause-and-effect* relationships of different outcomes.

Let's explore the concepts of lead/lag and cause and effect with a story. Imagine that you and some friends have a terrific new business idea. Ask yourself which of the following outcomes happens first:

- *Profits:* Profits enjoyed through dividends and/or stock appreciation by yourselves and other investors

- *Sales/customer satisfaction:* Purchase and satisfactory use of your products and/or services by customers

- *Salaries/skills:* Skilled and rewarded effort by the people of your new enterprise to create, sell, and support the products and services

This is not a trick question. You must see that profits cannot happen without sales to customers. And sales to customers cannot happen without skilled and rewarded effort by the people of the enterprise. So, salary and skill outcomes for people of the enterprise happen first.

Viewed this way, profits are *caused by* sales to customers and sales are *caused by* the productive efforts of people of the enterprise. Stated differently, outcomes like profits that indicate financial success *lag*—come as a result of—those outcomes regarding customer sales, service, and satisfaction, which, in turn, *lag* those outcomes associated with improving the skill and/or effectiveness of people of the enterprise. Stated in the reverse, outcomes regarding skilled and rewarded effort *lead* to outcomes measuring increases in value delivered to customers, which, in turn, *lead* to financial outcomes of concern to shareholders (see Figure 7.1).

Let's look, then, at the example of speed and financial performance from Chapter 6. Figure 7.2 repeats the arena mapping we constructed for each challenge. Notice that the metrics of the reengineering and Speed Now! initiatives primarily seek to improve outcomes that matter to customers. Consequently, the reengineering and Speed Now! outcomes will be leading indicators of financial performance. By delivering greater value to customers, the reengineering and Speed Now! teams are working toward greater financial returns for shareholders.

What about the Reengineering and Speed Now! Coordinating Teams? Their primary concern is to build the skill and effectiveness people need to deliver increased value to customers and financial results to shareholders. When these two Coordinating Teams succeed, people gain new skills and effectiveness. When those people, in turn, use their new skills and effectiveness to

Skilled/rewarded effort by people	causes leads to	Purchase and satisfied use by customers	causes leads to	Financial outcomes for shareholders

FIGURE 7.1 Lead/lag and cause and effect.

Arena mapping: Financial performance

Whole business		Function/dept.	Metrics		Jobs	Metrics
▪ Revenue (volume × price)		▪ Marketing	▪ Volume, price, revenue, cost		▪ Marketing	▪ Volume, price, revenue, cost
▪ Cost		▪ Operations	▪ Cost, volume		▪ Operations	▪ Volume, cost
▪ Profit		▪ Sales	▪ Volume, price, revenue, cost		▪ Sales	▪ Revenue, cost

Arena mapping: Speed

Whole business		Processes/subprocesses	Metrics		Individuals/teams	Metrics
▪ 'Be fastest'/qualitative alignment of speed/cycle times		▪ New product	▪ Cycle time, 'hit rate'		▪ Teams/individuals contributing to process performance	Same metrics as processes
▪ Customer satisfaction		▪ Order generation through fulfillment	▪ Cycle time, customer satisfaction		▪ Reengineering Coordinating Team	
		▪ Customer service	▪ Cycle time, customer satisfaction		▪ Reengineering Teams	Same metrics as initiatives
		Initiatives			▪ Speed Now! Coordinating Team	
		▪ Reengineering initiative	▪ Cycle time, 'hit rate'		▪ Speed Now! teams	
		▪ Speed Now! initiative	▪ Cycle time, customer satisfaction			

FIGURE 7.2 Arena mapping for financial performance and speed.

deliver increased value to customers, financial performance for shareholders also increases. As seen in Figure 7.3, the shareholder outcomes lag the customer outcomes, which, in turn, lag the efforts of the teams coordinating the two initiatives.

Figure 7.3, then, answers this question: How do the goals respecting speed relate to the goals respecting financial performance? In Figure 7.3, you see that outcomes measuring the skill and effectiveness of people of the enterprise lead to outcomes of increased speed for customers, which, in turn, lead to outcomes providing greater returns to shareholders. If, for example, you or your colleagues have personally committed to performance outcomes for both the financial challenge and the Speed Now! challenge, you can explain their connection as follows: *You are simultaneously working to meet this year's budget goals as well as participating in a Speed Now! team that will produce greater speed and customer satisfaction, which, in turn, will make it easier to meet financial targets both this year and in years to come.*

Concentrate for another moment on the preceding paragraph. In effect, it guides the alignment and integration of different performance challenges by asking you to locate the *primary* thrust of each challenge along the following continuum:

people outcomes → customer outcomes → shareholder outcomes

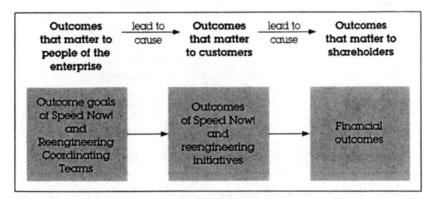

FIGURE 7.3 Cause and effect.

Figure 7.4 identifies the outcomes most often of *primary* concern in many of today's most pressing performance challenges. For example, customer outcomes are most often of primary concern in innovation-related initiatives, while effectiveness and satisfaction of the people of the enterprise are most often of primary

Performance challenge	Outcomes of primary concern
Alliances	Customers/shareholders
Core competencies	People of the enterprise/ customers
Customer service	Customers
Diversity	People of the enterprise
Electronic commerce	Customers
Growth	Shareholders
Innovation	Customers
Mergers/acquisitions	Customers/shareholders
Profitability	Shareholders
Reengineering	Customers/shareholders
Relationship-based marketing	Customers
Speed	Customers
Strategy	Customers/shareholders
Teams	People of the enterprise/ customers
Technology	Customers/shareholders
Total quality	Customers
Values/behaviors/best place to work	People of the enterprise

FIGURE 7.4 The primary thrust and concern of different performance challenges.

concern in "best place to work" initiatives. As always, there are exceptions to this pattern (in fact, a double choice appears for several kinds of initiatives).

You should use Figure 7.4 to identify the relationship among different performance challenges facing your organization. If, for example, your company currently emphasizes growth, profitability, innovation, speed, teams, and diversity, then the primary SMART outcome-based goals associated with each are aligned as follows:

People outcomes $\rightarrow$	Customer outcomes $\rightarrow$	Shareholder outcomes
Teams	Innovation	Growth
Diversity	Speed	Profitability

A visitor to your organization might ask, "How do the activities and goals of these six initiatives fit together?" You can answer in two ways. First, using the arena mapping emphasized in Chapter 6, you can explain how the goals for *any single challenge* are coordinated among the working arenas relevant to that challenge. Second, using the logic of the preceding table, you can observe how the six different efforts align with one another: "*Through teams and diversity outcomes, we are putting people of the enterprise in a position to deliver both innovation and speed outcomes to customers, which, in turn, will increase growth and profitability results for shareholders.*"

You can use this logic to integrate and focus your company's efforts. For example, the SMART outcome-based goals set in the teams initiative can purposefully reinforce the goals of the innovation and speed initiatives. Instead of consuming the resources of the teams initiative in "teams for the sake of teams," ask teams to set SMART outcome-based goals seeking specific innovation and speed outcomes within certain time frames. One such goal for the leaders of the teams initiative might be: "*Identify and help at least two dozen teams deliver significant improvements in speed and customer satisfaction over the next four months.*"

This tightly integrated and focused approach is too often missing from organizations. More typically, initiatives such as teams and diversity fail to integrate with the other performance challenges facing the organization. They get lost in worrying exclusively about teams and diversity for their own sake. Not only do they lose focus this way, but they tend to generate activity-based goals because they aren't really confident they know which outcomes are critical. As a consequence, people have difficulty articulating how the teams and diversity goals are aligned with innovation, speed, profitability, and growth goals. Everyone gets confused. People develop lists of goals, making certain to appear to be doing something for every important performance challenge. Then, when it comes time to prioritize, they inevitably focus their scarce time and energy on the goals that seem most important. And guess which goals win? That's right, the shareholder outcomes of growth and profitability. When pressed about their lack of progress against other challenges, people then complain, "We have too much to do. Management should stop adding so many new initiatives." In contrast, when people learn how to focus and integrate initiatives, they can make meaningful progress on all fronts with the resources and time available.

The Cycle of Sustainable Performance

Now let's turn to the task of aligning goals and outcomes that matter to different constituencies such as customers, shareholders, and the people of the enterprise. Earlier, we considered lead/lag and cause-and-effect relationships among performance outcomes for a start-up enterprise. Most organizations, however, are not start-ups; they are ongoing operations. This does not mean we reached the wrong conclusion about shareholder outcomes lagging customer outcomes, which, in turn, lag outcomes with respect to the rewards, skills, and effectiveness of people of the enterprise. The continuum depicted in Figure 7.1 also makes sense for going concerns. *But it doesn't go far enough.*

Why? Because it is too static and too linear. It fails to account for the reality that financial outcomes for shareholders not only *lag* customer and people outcomes, but also *lead* important outcomes for people of the enterprise and customers. To demonstrate this, imagine that a good friend calls to ask your advice about a job change. You know that your friend's company has suffered severe market share losses for the past five years and has remained profitable only because of a continuing series of cost-cutting efforts. You also know that the stress of repeated downsizing has taken a heavy toll on your friend, leaving him depressed and putting pressure on his marriage. He says he recently took a call from a headhunter and now has a job offer at General Electric Credit Corporation, which, he tells you, has produced double-digit revenue and profit growth for many years running. Moreover, the job is nearby and he won't have to move his family.

"What do you think I should do?", he asks.

"Are you kidding?," you declare with a big smile spreading across your face.

If ever there was a no-brainer, this is it. The point is simple. Financial performance that matters to shareholders *also matters to the people of the enterprise.* Your friend's choice of employer depends heavily on the comparative financial performance of his current employer and that of his prospective employer. As your friend pops the cork on a bottle of champagne over his good fortune, he is living proof that financial performance outcomes (established earlier as lagging other outcomes) are also *leading* indicators of the skill, rewards, and effectiveness of the people of the enterprise. *Financially sound and successful companies attract, reward, and retain skilled and effective people better than financially troubled ones do.*

Financially sound and successful companies also attract and retain customers better than financially troubled ones do. In other words, financial outcomes for shareholders are also leading indicators of outcomes for customers. To illustrate this, imagine that you are part of a team evaluating bids among various software and hardware vendors. Along with other important criteria, your team will pay close attention to the financial strength of each bidder because you know that information technology evolves quickly and you don't want your company to be stuck with a vendor that goes bust or cannot afford to upgrade its products.

The *linear* picture in Figure 7.1 is too static and unidirectional. It misses the *cyclical interdependence* of lead/lag and cause-and-effect relationships among outcomes that matter to customers, shareholders, and the people of the enterprise. Figure 7.1 suggests that, as in Rome, all roads lead to financial outcomes and only financial outcomes. The cycle of sustainable performance (Figure 7.5) introduced in Chapter 1 is superior to the linear depiction of lead/lag relationships for several reasons:

- *It depicts a philosophy for never ending success.* Figure 7.5 presents a principled view of how organizations can succeed *forever.* Does it guarantee such a result? Of course not. But the logic for sustainable, open-ended success is made explicit: "Shareholders who provide skills, opportunities, and rewards to people of the enterprise who deliver value to

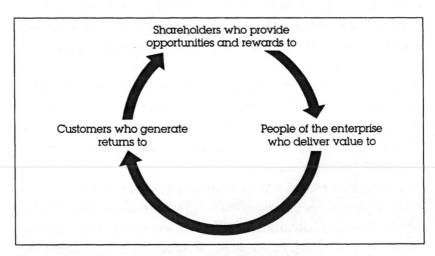

FIGURE 7.5 The cycle of sustainable performance.

customers at a price that generates returns to shareholders who provide skills, opportunities, and rewards to people of the enterprise who deliver value to customers at a price that generates returns to shareholders who. . . ." Organizations that act on this logic ensure that their strategic, organizational, technological, and operational choices make sense to all constituencies that matter.

■ *It is truly balanced and integrated.* The linear depiction in Figure 7.1 highlights why organizations must pay attention to the people of the enterprise and customers as well as shareholders, and to nonfinancial as well as financial outcomes. In that sense, any scorecard that uses Figure 7.1 is multidimensional. But such scorecards are neither truly balanced nor integrated. Instead, the logic favors shareholders because outcomes that matter to the people of the enterprise and customers are but means to an end—and that end is financial performance. The multidimensional view in Figure 7.1 *is* an advance on the classic belief that the only performance that matters is financial; it at least makes room for other kinds of outcomes. But it achieves only an incremental improvement. In contrast, the cycle of sustainable performance in Figure 7.5 is truly balanced and integrated. None of the constituencies—shareholders, people of the enterprise, customers—are favored; none are "more equal than others." Instead, the objective is to create harmonized performance that *sustainably* benefits all three constituencies in a dynamic and open-ended manner.

■ *It encourages the use of "both/and" goals.* Recall from Chapter 4 the benefits of putting "both/and" creative tension into specific outcome-based goals. People excel when challenged to deliver performance in two or more competing dimensions ("*both* reduce costs *and* increase customer satisfaction") versus only one ("reduce costs"). The performance cycle in Figure 7.5 demands such creative tension.

Any organization on the planet can (for some period) increase returns to shareholders *or* invest in people's skills and opportunities *or* improve value to customers. But only the greatest, most enduring enterprises can *both* increase value for shareholders *and* increase the rewards, skills, and opportunities for the people of the enterprise *and* increase value for customers.

■ *It permits the integration of strategic alliances into the score-card.*   Organizations form strategic alliances to take advantage of opportunities to better serve one or more chosen groups of customers. Figure 7.5 is easily modified to capture the performance intent of such alliances. As Figure 7.6 indicates, people from each of the allied enterprises must collaborate to deliver outcomes that matter to customers if their respective companies' shareholders are to benefit, and if they and the rest of their colleagues are to continue to enjoy skills, opportunities, and rewards.

■ *It translates to the government and nonprofit sectors.*   Figures 7.7 and 7.8 convert the cycle of sustainable performance into terms relevant to government and nonprofit

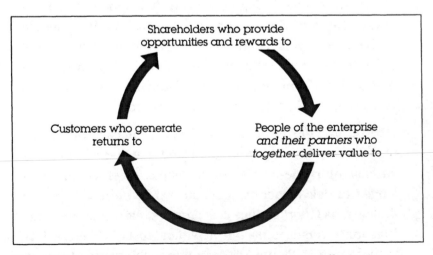

FIGURE 7.6 The cycle of sustainable performance/alliances.

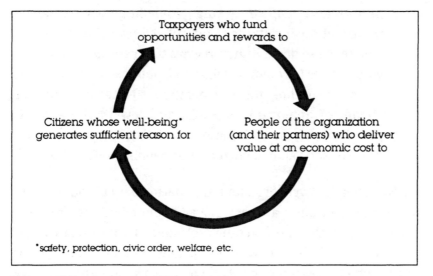

FIGURE 7.7 The cycle of sustainable performance: government organizations.

enterprises. Interestingly, people in such organizations often have trouble understanding and integrating financial and economic challenges into a total picture alongside nonfinancial challenges (the reverse pattern of many organizations in the for-profit sector). The reinforcing cycle of

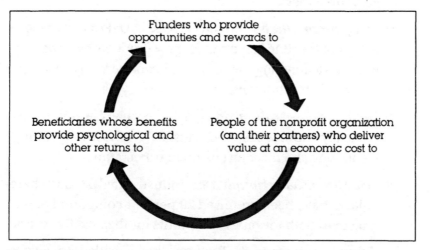

FIGURE 7.8 The cycle of sustainable performance: nonprofit organizations.

performance helps by asking people in governmental and nonprofit organizations to articulate how value, price, and cost relate to one another in ways that can sustainably provide returns (psychological, social, political, and economic) to those funding the organization so that a continuing stream of opportunities, skills, and rewards flows to the people of the enterprise and so that, in turn, they can continue to add value to citizens and beneficiaries, and so on.

By using the cycle of sustainable performance, you and your colleagues can paint a tight, logically connected picture of the challenges, goals, and outcomes relevant to your organization's success, regardless of how many or how different those performance challenges might be. And you can also identify initiatives and goals that don't make sense in the overall picture. To illustrate this, consider the following efforts under way at a major U.S.-based industrial products company ("USProducts"):

- *Global expansion:* More than 80 percent of USProducts' revenues are U.S.-based. Opportunities exist to shift the balance to 50 percent U.S./50 percent non-U.S. over the next three years.

- *Reengineering the new product process:* USProducts believes it can cut the time to market for new products by 70 percent, while also doubling the hit rate of commercially successful new product introductions.

- *Total customer satisfaction:* The company wants to dramatically improve customer satisfaction and loyalty through identifying and meeting customer expectations.

- *20/20 financial performance:* Industry analysts and shareholders have been promised 20 percent compound annual growth in both revenues and profits for the next five years.

- *Talent imperative:* USProducts has decided to aggressively develop, reward, and retain people.

- *Team performance:* Team skills and performance are being stressed at all levels of the company, from the front lines to the executive suite.

Figure 7.9 depicts how these efforts relate to one another. You can see how the outcomes associated with the talent imperative and team performance initiatives reinforce customer outcomes associated with global expansion, new product process, and total customer satisfaction, which, in turn, will produce financial outcomes that matter to shareholders. Moreover, you should observe that the financial outcomes for shareholders help produce even greater opportunities, rewards, and skills for the people of the enterprise to continue applying teams and talent as well as skills related to reengineering, globalization, and total customer satisfaction to continue delivering 20/20 financial performance into the future.

The six efforts, then, seem to make sense. Now let's ask whether the CEO of USProducts should announce any of the following additional performance initiatives:

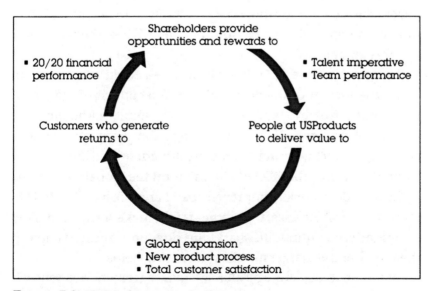

FIGURE 7.9 USProducts: six challenges.

- A merger with a company whose business is entirely U.S.-based

- A strategic alliance that outsources both U.S. and non-U.S. transportation, warehousing, and delivery logistics to an established global supplier

- An across-the-board, 25 percent head count reduction over the next 18 months

The merger makes no sense. On its face, it kills the global expansion aspirations of this company. More subtly, it will seriously slow down and possibly kill the reengineering of the new product process as well as the talent imperative because progress toward each would have to wait for postmerger integration efforts to conclude. Similarly, the across-the-board head count reduction clashes with the coordinated direction and strategy of this company. The original six initiatives paint an overall picture of a company trying to expand, deepen, and enrich the value it delivers to its customers, shareholders, and people. Success requires serious risk taking by people at USProducts as well as medium- to long-term investment in people's skills and opportunities. It defies intellectual and emotional credibility to inject into this picture the prospect that one in four people will lose their jobs over the next 18 months!

No one, from the CEO to the front lines, could make sense of either the merger or the downsizing in the context of the rest of the six initiatives arrayed around the performance cycle shown in Figure 7.9. Yes, the CEO could change the company's course, choosing to pursue a fundamentally different overall direction for USProducts (e.g., the CEO might abandon the global aspirations in favor of dramatically improved speed and profitability in U.S. markets—in which case, the merger might make sense). But if the six initiatives continue to shape the direction of the company, then neither the merger nor the downsizing helps.

In contrast, the strategic alliance makes tremendous sense. It should hasten results toward the company's global aspirations, while also introducing uniformity to the customer experience that would improve total customer satisfaction. Assuming that the economics of outsourcing are favorable, this alliance also should support the company's 20/20 goals. The outsourcing will also require effective teaming with the strategic partner, thereby providing more opportunities for team performance.

Aligning Goals over Time— Simultaneous versus Sequential Outcomes

We can now discuss the final piece of the goal alignment puzzle, namely, the *time frames* within which performance outcomes are accomplished. Doing so requires only that we pose a single, determinative question: *Are the time frames in which any given set of performance outcomes is to be completed simultaneous or sequential?*

Sometimes, one or more performance outcomes are achieved in the same time frame. They are simultaneous with one another. Sometimes, outcomes in one time frame lead to outcomes in a later or longer time frame. These are sequential. Consider, for example, the customer satisfaction, 20/20, talent imperative, and teams initiatives at USProducts. You and I might be on a team seeking to build an electronic data interchange link with BigCo, a customer of USProducts. Let's say our team has established the following SMART outcome-based goal: "*Over the next eight weeks, use electronic data interchange to shorten product order through delivery time to BigCo by 90 percent, while simultaneously eliminating all order- and delivery-related defects.*" As the goal indicates, the reductions in time and defects are simultaneous.

Imagine that by succeeding with this goal, we know we will also *simultaneously* learn a lot about the team discipline and (based on analysis we have done) reduce USProducts' order and delivery costs to BigCo by 20 percent, producing a 6 percent increase in profit margin for the BigCo account. With all this in mind, those of us on this BigCo EDI team can explain how our SMART outcome-based goals contribute to several of USProducts' performance challenges and constituency outcomes. Through our electronic data interchange project, we are contributing to each of the following over the next eight weeks:

- Improvement in BigCo's customer satisfaction
- Profit improvement in BigCo's account (a contribution to the 20/20 initiative)
- Personal growth and development
- Contribution to applying the team discipline throughout USProducts

Notice that the outcomes associated with this project happen *simultaneously*, that is, in parallel and concurrently. In the same eight weeks it takes to complete the specific improvement in BigCo's customer satisfaction, we also achieve the stated profit improvement in BigCo's account, an advancement in our personal skills related to teaming, and our contribution to the outcomes of the teams.

Sometimes outcomes happen sequentially. Consider USProducts' new product reengineering, 20/20, teams, and customer satisfaction initiatives. This time, let's say that you and I are members of a cross-functional reengineering design team asked to achieve the following outcomes: "*Within the next three months, deliver a redesigned new product development process that, over the ensuing 18 months, will double the commercial success rate of USProducts' new products, while simultaneously cutting time to market by 70 percent.*"

Assuming that our reengineering design team succeeds, the time it takes us to complete the design aspects of our reengineering challenge is three months. In contrast, our time to completion for contributing to the 20/20 and customer satisfaction initiatives extends over 18 months. Now, let's pose three questions about goal alignment:

1. *How do our reengineering design team's goals align against the key performance challenges of USProducts?* Within three months, our team will have redesigned the new product development process and, thereby, contributed to the reengineering, talent, and teams initiatives. Our contribution at the end of three months will *sequentially* lead over the following 18 months to a variety of contributions that matter to USProducts' reengineering effort (double success rate in 70 percent shorter time), total customer satisfaction (better products, faster time to market), and 20/20 performance (more successful new products). Assuming that the redesign of the new product process relies on increased teaming and process management skills, then the work done in the first three months also will sequentially lead to outcomes for the talent and teams initiatives over the ensuing 18 months.

2. *How do the reengineering design team's goals align against USProducts' critical constituencies?* In the first three months, the efforts of the reengineering design team to redesign the new product process primarily benefit the people of the enterprise. Why? Because the team itself, as well as others who work with the team, will have seized an opportunity to enrich their skills at teaming, customer orientation, reengineering, and process management. Outcomes that matter to customers and shareholders take effect over the ensuing 18 months as the redesigned new product process delivers more successful products faster. Accordingly, the outcomes for people of the enterprise *sequentially* lead to outcomes that matter to customers and shareholders.

3. *How do the reengineering design team's goals align with goals of other working arenas such as the BigCo EDI team?* Assume that we gathered together the people on the reengineering design team and BigCo EDI team and

asked them how their goals aligned with one another and with USProducts' critical challenges and constituencies. Through describing their SMART outcome-based goals in terms of simultaneous versus sequential time frames, the teams would learn the following:

- Each was contributing to the total customer satisfaction, 20/20, talent imperative, and teams initiatives at USProducts, although the time to completion of the various contributions ranged across 8 weeks, 3 months, and 21 months.

- Each was contributing to outcomes that matter to customers, shareholders, and people of the enterprise, although the BigCo EDI team's outcomes occurred simultaneously, while the reengineering design team's outcomes occurred sequentially (first for people of the enterprise, and then for customers and shareholders).

- Neither team was doing anything that contradicted or got in the way of the other team. Indeed, further opportunities for tighter alignment might arise. For example, the reengineering design team might recognize an opportunity to include people from BigCo as part of customer review efforts early in the new product process. Or the team might choose to specify linkage to electronic data interchange as a key requirement of new products.

By identifying when outcomes happen simultaneously as opposed to sequentially, you can round out your understanding of cause-and-effect relationships among goals and challenges. The key, as illustrated by the USProducts examples, lies in understanding *the time to completion of any particular challenge and how that time to completion relates to the time frames necessary to deliver outcomes in other challenges and for other constituencies.*

Exercise 7.1: Cause and Effect

Write down the set of programs, initiatives, or performance challenges currently going on within your organization. Using Figure 7.4 as a reference, agree among yourselves about the primary thrust of each of these challenges or initiatives. Don't take the suggestions in Figure 7.4 as required. Rather, make sure that you debate and agree on what you believe to be the primary thrust of each of the challenges. Once you have done so, use the following table to make sense out of the overall picture:

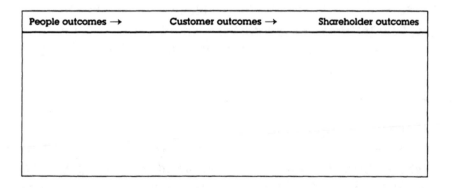

People outcomes →	Customer outcomes →	Shareholder outcomes

Exercise 7.2: Creating Reinforcing SMART Outcomes

In Exercise 7.1, you and your colleagues identified the primary thrust of different performance challenges and initiatives in your organization. Take a moment to concentrate on the challenges that primarily concern people outcomes. Such initiatives might include teams, diversity, best place to work, values and behaviors, culture change, core competencies, centers of competency, and centers of excellence. Try to create SMART outcome-based goals for these initiatives that *explicitly reinforce* the customer and shareholder initiatives you have also identified. An example of an explicitly integrated and reinforcing goal was provided earlier in this chapter: "*Identify and help at least two dozen teams deliver significant improvements in speed and customer satisfaction over the next four months.*" You might use Exercise 4.2 and Exercise 5.3 to help you.

Exercise 7.3: Tell a Performance Story

Consider the cycle of sustainable performance in Figure 7.5. Place each of the performance challenges or initiatives you identified in Exercise 7.1 on the part of the performance cycle that makes the most sense to you. See Figure 7.9 for an illustration of this. Once you have arrayed the challenges or initiatives around the performance cycle, use the picture to tell a story about how your organization is seeking to create sustainable performance. Discuss among yourselves the coherence, logic, and completeness of this story. Is anything missing? If so, what? Are there initiatives or challenges under way or being considered that don't make sense? Which ones and why?

Exercise 7.4: Arena Mapping and Time to Completion

Do an arena mapping for a major performance challenge or initiative your organization has on its agenda (see exercises in Chapter 6 to help). Once you have completed this mapping, create SMART outcome-based goals for each of the significant working arenas identified. Discuss among yourselves the time frames required to complete the various goals identified. Based on your answers, identify those goals that can be achieved simultaneously versus those that must be achieved sequentially. (This exercise may take up to a full day to complete.)

Exercise 7.5: Avoid Mindless Goal Proliferation by Cascading the Logic of Sustainable Performance instead of Cascading Specific Goals

Before describing this exercise, I need to provide some background. Many organizations that have adopted the balanced scorecard approach have really only figured out how to set goals for all constituencies (customers, shareholders, people of the enterprise, partners) at the whole organization level (whole corporation or business unit). They have not figured out how to set goals for balanced performance among functions, processes, initiatives, teams and individuals, and other working arenas.

Here is what typically happens in such organizations. After the leaders set a series of goals that matter to shareholders, customers, and the people of the enterprise, they ask their direct reports to set goals that contribute to each. Those direct reports then set a series of specific goals for each goal the top leaders have set. For example, if the top leaders have set 6 specific goals, each of their direct reports then sets 2 or 3 goals that contribute to each of the 6. If there are a total of, say, 25 direct reports, and an average of 3 goals for each of the 6 top goals, then there are a total of 25 times 3 times 6, or 300 goals.

Now, the 25 direct reports ask their direct reports to start setting goals that will contribute to these 300 goals. And so on. In a large, multilayered organization, by the time everyone has participated in this cascading of goals, there could easily be tens of thousands of goals throughout the organization—and mass confusion and chaos. This practice of cascading top goals also leads to a tremendous number of activity-based goals as well as goals limited to formally designated working arenas such as functions, departments, and individuals.

To avoid this trap, I recommend that organizations pay more attention to cascading *the logic of the cycle of sustainable performance than to cascading specific goals.* As we have examined in this chapter, the cycle of sustainable performance helps you identify the primary thrust of your efforts and, thereby, see how different efforts relate to one another—to see how you can "tell a performance story." If asked, anyone in any working arena can tell such a story by using the frameworks and tools of this book. For example, as we reviewed in the USProducts story of this chapter, the leaders of USProducts can tell the following performance story: "*Through the talent imperative and team performance we are going to shift the balance of our revenues from 80/20 U.S./non-U.S. to 50/50, cut our time to market for new products by 70 percent, while doubling the hit rate, and dramatically improve customer satisfaction so that we can deliver on our 20/20 financial performance promises.*"

We also reviewed two examples at the team level, each of which could tell their own performance story. For example, the BigCo EDI team might say they were "using the team discipline and electronic data interchange to shorten delivery time to BigCo by 90 percent, while also eliminating all defects so that they produced cost reductions and margin improvements that contributed to the overall 20/20 financial goals of the company." The performance goals and performance story of the BigCo EDI team certainly relates well to the overall direction of USProducts. In fact, it relates much more effectively than any set of goals the team might have generated if it had been part of an overall "cascading of goals" effort.

Thus, the purpose of this exercise is to help you learn how to cascade the logic of storytelling around the cycle of sustainable performance instead of cascading specific goals. To do so, gather a group of colleagues and identify no more than a handful of working arenas to which you contribute. Make sure those working arenas are relevant to the performance challenges facing your organization. Together with your colleagues, spend the time needed to:

1. Articulate the overall performance story of your organization (Exercises 7.1 through 7.3 can help).

2. Identify the working arenas to which you and your colleagues contribute.

3. For each of these working arenas, describe how the performance outcomes in those arenas contribute to the organization's overall performance story.

4. Spell out SMART outcome-based goals for each of these working arenas.

5. Based on these goals and how they matter to the whole organization, tell a performance story for each of the working arenas.

CHAPTER 8

Small Group Performance

Working Group versus Team Management Disciplines

Understanding the Two Disciplines for Small Group Performance

All the work and, therefore, all the performance of organizations ultimately is achieved by individuals and teams. In this chapter, we turn our attention to the two management disciplines needed to ensure that individuals and teams succeed. Jon Katzenbach and I first distinguished these two disciplines—the working group discipline and the team discipline—in our book, *The Wisdom of Teams*. The working group discipline, the much better known and practiced of the two, delivers performance that depends on individual contributions. In contrast, the team discipline must be used when performance outcomes require the combination of multiple skills and perspectives of two or more people working together.

Let's first review the familiar working group discipline. Its practice includes the following:

- The leader of the group (the boss) makes and communicates a decision about how best to achieve performance.

- The leader of the group assigns individual responsibilities and goals.

- The leader of the group monitors the progress of each individual.

- The leader of the group evaluates overall group progress and makes adjustments as needed to group direction as well as individual assignments, responsibilities, and goals.

- The leader of the group encourages sharing of ideas and best practices.

- The leader of the group is in control.

For example, imagine that you are the manager of a sales region for a restaurant supply company. You have 10 salespeople in your region. This year's goal is to grow revenues by 10 percent and increase the number of accounts from 150 to 180. As the year begins, you gather your group together and discuss the goals, why they matter to the company, and how best the group might achieve them. You assign each of the 10 salespeople their individual goals, being careful to ensure that, if each of the 10 succeeds, the sum of their individual performances will surpass the overall goal. You tell the group there is an extra bonus associated with exceeding the target revenue and new account goals.

As the year proceeds, you gather your group regularly to monitor individual performance and to encourage the sharing of ideas, best practices, and other information. You closely attend to overall progress. When you become concerned about any of the salespeople falling short, you spend time with them to see if you can help. In addition, you adjust goals for salespeople if necessary to ensure that overall performance will at least meet the group's revenue and new accounts targets.

Throughout the entire year's effort, you encourage openness and sharing of ideas, you listen carefully to each of your people, and you work to respond and help them succeed. Let us say, then, that you are the ideal, terrific boss. Notice, though, that at the center of your managerial efforts is one unquestioned and critical reality: *You are in control.*

This principle of control is what most distinguishes the working group discipline from the team discipline. In the team discipline, the aspiration is for the team to be in control, not the boss. In contrast, in the working group discipline, everyone throughout the organization expects and wants the boss to be in control. The boss's boss wants the boss to be in control. The boss wants to be in control. And, more important, the people working for the boss want the boss to be in control. The efficiency and effectiveness with which performance outcomes are accomplished depend on the boss being in control.

The working group discipline works. It has been practiced, honed, and perfected over more than 200 years since Adam Smith first identified the division of labor as central to economic performance. And as we emphasize in *The Wisdom of Teams,* there is nothing bad about choosing the working group discipline, with all of its command and control characteristics, *so long as the desired performance of the small group is best achieved in that manner.*

By the way, knowing that the working group discipline *can* work does not ensure that it *will* work. Most of us know the difference between managers who practice it well and those who practice it poorly. The leaders who are best at this discipline work hard to gather input from their subordinates and others, to ensure that decisions are fact-based, to insist on openness and sharing, and to listen persistently and be responsive. In addition, the best working group leaders put the lessons of this book to use by:

- *Shaping SMART outcome-based goals for the group as well as for each individual.*   Effective working group leaders avoid activity-based goals. They make certain to set outcome-based goals for the group and each individual that are specific, measurable, aggressive yet achievable, relevant to the challenge at hand, and time-bound. The goals they articulate use the good goal grammar outlined in Exercise 3.4.

- *Selecting metrics that are relevant to the challenge at hand.* In the preceding sales force example, the selection of metrics was easy. Such is not always the case. Effective working group leaders openly discuss and gather input on the obstacles to using unfamiliar, nonfinancial, and sometimes qualitative metrics. Such leaders then make decisions about which metrics to use and stick with those metrics long enough to learn from them.

- *Pursuing the SMART cycle of performance.* The best working group bosses set SMART outcome-based goals; pursue them; evaluate, monitor, and adjust; and then start the whole cycle over again. They insist on openness and sharing so that everyone in the group learns and progresses.

- *Building both creative and personal tension into group and individual goals.* Effective working group leaders build creative tension into goals by applying the "both/and" logic examined in Chapter 4. For example, they select metrics that demand improvement in both effort (speed and cost) and return on effort (on-spec/expec and positive yields) by using the four yardsticks. Moreover, the best working group bosses instill personal tension through using open forums attended by both internal and external customers and suppliers for the declaration of goals as well as follow-up, monitoring, and adjustment.

- *Making sure each person in the group understands how his or her personal contributions make a difference to the performance of the whole company.* By identifying the working arenas needed to meet any given challenge and then ensuring that the SMART outcomes assigned to individuals in those arenas line up with the goals of the rest of the organization, working group leaders help people understand how their individual performance fits into the big picture. Moreover, by applying the logic of the cycle of sustainable performance, effective working group bosses help themselves and others see how their performance matters to customers, shareholders, the people of the enterprise (including themselves), and other constituencies.

With these criteria in mind, let's take another look at your effectiveness as the sales manager in our example. As mentioned, you have already demonstrated that you are very effective at using the working group discipline to deliver performance. Congratulations! But you could have managed in a way that delivered even better performance. How?

Assume that you converted the revenue and new account goals into SMART outcomes for the group and for each individual. However, you did not instill these goals with any creative tension. You might have done so by adding a speed goal to shorten the cycle time needed to get new accounts up and running. Instead of the goal to "add 30 new accounts this year," you could have challenged your group to help you "*add 30 new accounts this year while simultaneously reducing the time from sign-up to first satisfied use of product by 75 percent.*" In addition, you could have added metrics and goals that matter as much to customers and the people of your company as to shareholders. For example, you might have added some requirements regarding customer expectations and satisfaction.

In taking such steps, you would figure out that the working arenas relevant to success stretched beyond the capacity of your individual salespeople acting on their own. For example, to reduce the cycle time of new account opening would demand a review of the new account process, a working arena involving people from accounting, distribution, logistics, and sales (and, possibly, from one or more manufacturers represented by your restaurant supply company). If you added this speed and customer satisfaction outcome to your performance mix, you would discover that the working group discipline could not achieve it. Instead, you would need to apply the team discipline.

Why? Because improving the speed and customer satisfaction associated with the new account opening process demands the real-time integration of multiple skills and perspectives of people from sales, accounting, distribution, logistics, and possibly one or more manufacturers. As the head of a single sales region, you have neither the authority nor the experience to effectively apply the working group discipline to this goal. Instead, you need to assemble a team whose members then must use the following six elements of the team discipline to achieve their goals:

1. *Small number.* While not impossible, groups that number more than 10 to 12 people find it extremely difficult to apply the team discipline. In fact, such groups tend to break down their goals into subgoals and team up in smaller units to accomplish them. Through keeping their numbers small, teams are more likely to reach the kind of common understanding and agreement required to take full advantage of individual, functional, experiential, skill, and hierarchical differences.

2. *Complimentary skills.* Teams must have the mix of multiple skills and perspectives needed to meet the performance challenge at hand. Typically, teams draw from three families of skills: (a) technical and functional, (b) problem-solving and decision-making, and (c) interpersonal. As *The Wisdom of Teams* explains, successful teams typically develop the full complement of required skills *after* getting started. Indeed, it is the rare team that has all the right skills in place at the beginning.

3. *Common purpose.* Together with common goals and a commonly agreed-upon working approach, common purpose provides the litmus test of whether the team, as opposed to the boss, is in control. Teams cannot perform as teams unless their purpose, goals, and approach are shaped and owned *by the team*. Purpose provides the meaning and direction to the team. Purpose engenders a sense of pride, responsibility, and enthusiasm.

Common purpose, like common goals and a common working approach, does not require 100 percent consensus. Indeed, disagreement is one of the sources of excellent team performance. Typically, if you need different skills and perspectives to achieve performance, then you also need the disagreements and debates triggered by those differences. To reach common purpose, common goals, and a common working approach requires that, when there is disagreement, each party to the disagreement can articulate to the other party's satisfaction the other party's point of view. Put differently, if you and I disagree, I don't have to agree with you but I do have to understand your point of view, and vice versa. Once this level of mutual understanding is accomplished, common purpose, goals, and working approach demand that the team use some mechanism for making a choice and moving forward.

4. *Common performance goals.* Purposes provide the inspiration and emotional energy required for team performance. Goals provide the specific, concrete, and measurable outcomes that teams must achieve on their path to success. As such, team goals must be SMART, they must be outcome-based, and they must lend themselves to the iterative cycle of goal setting, progress, evaluation, monitoring, and adjustment. Moreover, team goals must fit the working arenas relevant to the team (see Chapter 5). A single account relationship team, for example, could not deliver a 10 percent sales increase for an entire company. It could, however, set and deliver outcomes that fit the account for which the team is responsible.

5. *Commonly agreed-upon working approach.* Teams must define and divide up the work required to achieve their goals. Effective teams develop a common understanding of three different categories of work. First, and most familiar, teams identify and assign responsibilities for the technical, func-

tional, and problem-solving work that needs to get done. Second, teams figure out how best to do the administrative work that nearly always gets done by the boss in a working group situation. Third, teams develop and agree on norms of behavior for how to work together including such conventions as thinking out of the box, fact-based decision making, mechanisms for decision making, constructive listening, feedback, candor, dealing with conflict, and having fun.

6. *Mutual accountability.* No team can succeed without holding itself mutually accountable *as a team* for its purpose, goals, and working approach. Mutual accountability does not displace individual accountability; individuals remain accountable for their individual contributions. But mutual accountability is what separates team performance from working group performance. People who are part of effective teams know in their hearts and minds that only the team can succeed or fail. When a performance challenge truly demands the team discipline, then no amount of individual success matters unless the team, as a team, succeeds.

Mutual accountability emerges from the mutual commitment and trust required by the team discipline. Through developing and committing to a common purpose, common goals, and a common working approach, the team controls its own performance and destiny. When the team is in control, people on the team know they must trust one another to be candid, work hard, help out, and do whatever is needed to meet the team's goal.

The team discipline is a managerial approach that delivers team performance. Like the working group discipline, the team discipline can be applied well or poorly. If you are part of a group applying the team discipline to meet a particular performance challenge, use the questions in Figure 8.1 to help monitor your progress. In addition, use the SMART cycle of performance discussed in Chapter 3 to pursue, evaluate, and adjust as your team

1. **Teams should be the right size.**
   Can you convene easily and frequently?
   Can you communicate with all members easily and often?
   Are your discussions open and interactive for all members?
   Does each member understand everyone else's roles and skills?
   Do you need other people to achieve your ends? (Has anyone been mistakenly excluded?)
   Are subteams possible or necessary?

2. **Teams should have adequate levels of complementary skills.**
   Are three categories of skills represented—functional/technical, problem-solving/decision-making, and interpersonal?
   Does each member have the potential to advance his or her skills to the level required by the team's purpose and goals?
   Are any skills that are critical to team performance missing or underrepresented?
   Are the team members, individually and collectively, willing to spend time to help themselves and others learn and develop new skills?
   Can new or supplemental skills be introduced as needed?

3. **Teams should have a truly meaningful overall purpose.**
   Does the team's purpose support the organization's purpose?
   Is it a team purpose, as distinguished from merely an official purpose, or just one individual's purpose? For example, has the leader expropriated the group's original purpose?
   Do all the members understand the team's purpose? Can they articulate it in concrete terms the same way?
   Do members define the team's purpose vigorously in discussions with people who aren't team members?
   Do members frequently refer to the team's purpose and explore its implications?
   Do members feel the team's purpose is important and that the group's success will be memorable?

4. **Teams should have specific goals.**
   Are the goals clear, simple, and measurable? If not precisely measurable, can their achievements be assessed?
   Are the goals realistic as well as ambitious? Do they allow for small wins along the way?
   Do the goals call for a set of concrete work products?
   Is the relative importance of each goal and its order of priority clear to all team members?
   Do all members agree with the goals, their relative importance, and the way in which achieving them is to be measured?

5. **Teams should have a clear working approach.**
   Is the approach concrete, clear, understood, and agreed to by everyone? Will it result in the achievement of the objectives?

(continued)

FIGURE 8.1 How well are you applying the team discipline?

Will it capitalize on the skills of the members?

Does the approach require all members to contribute equivalent amounts of work?

Does the approach provide for open interactions, fact-based problem solving, and results-based evaluation?

Does it provide for modification and improvement over time?

Are fresh input and perspective systematically sought and added—for example, through information and analysis, new members, and senior sponsors?

6. **Teams should have a sense of mutual accountability.**

Are the members individually and jointly accountable for the team's purpose, goals, approach, and work products?

Can you and do you measure progress against specific goals?

Do all members feel responsible for all measures?

Are the members clear on the contributions for which they're individually responsible, and those for which the team is jointly responsible?

Is there a clear understanding that "only the team can fail"?

FIGURE 8.1 *Continued.*

moves forward. The team discipline is more difficult to use than the working group discipline. It is much harder for a group of people to be in control as a team than for a boss to be in control. Nevertheless, if you can achieve your performance challenge only through the integration of multiple skills and perspectives of two or more people working together, then you must use the team discipline, difficult or not.

The pitfalls associated with the team discipline reinforce the importance of making your choice of disciplines carefully. The choice depends entirely on performance. Let me emphatically repeat a message from *The Wisdom of Teams: The team discipline is about performance, not the desire to be a team!* The least likely way to become a team is to set as your primary objective, either explicitly or implicitly, "let's be a team." Performance goals, commonly understood and pursued, are what create teams. And, as illustrated by this chapter's sales region example, you must use SMART outcome-based performance goals as your guide for choosing between the team discipline and the working group discipline. Thus, in that example, it made sense to choose the working group discipline for the revenue and new account goals and the team discipline for the new account speed goal. The question you must ask is not, "Should we be a team or a working group?" but rather "In light of the performance goals we have set, *when* should we use the team discipline and *when* should we use the working group discipline?" Both disciplines are relevant to the challenges faced by people in today's organizations. Performance outcomes determine when to use one and when to use the other.

Use a Performance Agenda to Achieve Both Individual and Team Performance in Your Small Group

The working group and team approaches are managerial disciplines for achieving desired performance, not types of organizational units or entities. The question you and your colleagues should ask is, "For any particular performance challenge and outcome, will we more likely succeed by using the working group discipline or the team discipline?" When considered in this light, most small groups in most of today's organizations, whether at the front lines or in the executive suite, find they must use a mix of both disciplines to accomplish the outcomes on their agenda.

I have developed a management tool called the *performance agenda* to help you and your colleagues succeed in making and using the best choices. Figure 8.2 lays out the format for such an agenda. Performance agendas facilitate a pragmatic, performance-driven approach to prioritization. Here's how performance agendas work.

List the Performance Challenges Confronting Your Small Group

Take the time to make as complete a list as possible. In doing so, remember that you are identifying only those challenges to which the people in your small group will make a contribution. As you consider all the programs, strategies, initiatives, and projects happening in your organization, ask yourselves whether the peo-

Challenges we are resourcing	SMART outcome-based goals	Which discipline?	Responsibility (names)

Other challenges we face, but are not resourcing	Illustrative outcomes that would indicate success

FIGURE 8.2 Performance agenda for small group.

ple in your group participate in any working arenas required for success. For example, in the sales region example in this chapter, you would add the new account cycle time reduction challenge to your performance agenda because it requires participation by some people in your group.

Convert Each Challenge into One or More SMART Outcome-Based Goals That Would Indicate Success

Use the tools, techniques, and exercises of Chapters 1 through 5 to articulate SMART outcome-based goals for the performance challenges on your agenda. Ask yourselves how these goals line up with the efforts and goals of other parts of your organization. Also ask how the SMART outcome-based goals you set would benefit all constituencies—customers, shareholders, and people of the enterprise.

Determine Which of These Performance Challenges and Outcomes Your Group Will Staff

There are two questions your group must answer with respect to each challenge on your agenda. First, will you assign one or more people responsibility for achieving the challenge and outcome in question? Second, will you expect those who are assigned to devote enough time and resources in the current time period to succeed? How you answer these questions will pragmatically determine your group's performance priorities. Note that no matter how important and significant a challenge might be, if your group cannot or will not assign any current resources to it or if, in doing so, your group does not expect the people assigned to credibly and significantly progress toward the outcomes in question, then your group is not really trying to meet that challenge in the current time frame.

The first of these questions is straightforward. Either you have assigned resources or you haven't. It is the second that demands candor. In my experience, groups too often officially fool themselves and others with unrealistic assignments that, in their hearts, everyone knows are insufficient to make any difference. Don't let your group waste its own time and effort in this fashion.

Draw a Line between Those Challenges That Are Sufficiently Resourced and Those That Are Not

This line becomes a critical management tool. Small groups with which I have worked quickly learn that challenges *above the line* are those that are important and are being sufficiently resourced while those *below the line* are important but not currently resourced. Notice that both those above the line and those below the line are important.

Prioritization efforts too often fail because of false distinctions about importance. Clearly, there are occasions when groups face challenges that are unimportant. But that is the exception, not the rule, in today's turbulent and competitive organizational environment. Far more often, nearly all of the challenges faced by groups are important. Thus, in using performance agendas to manage yourselves, I suggest that you avoid the important-versus-unimportant snare. Instead, recognize that, like most people in most organizations, you do not have unlimited resources, time, and attention. You should make your choices for what goes above the line on the logic of resources and seriousness of effort expected, not the relative importance of the challenges. Moreover, as discussed below, by keeping all of the relevant performance challenges on your agenda, you put yourselves in an excellent position to achieve those challenges that are resourced and then move other challenges above the line when resources and serious effort become available to them.

For Challenges above the Line, Determine Whether the Outcomes Demand the Working Group or the Team Discipline

For each performance challenge and the related SMART outcome-based goals above the line, ask yourselves whether success depends more on the working group discipline or the team discipline. Are you more likely to achieve the goal through the assignment and completion of individual goals? Or does success demand the integration of multiple skills and perspectives of two or more people working collaboratively in real time? After discussing, debating, and deciding which discipline makes the most sense, be sure to record your conclusion next to the relevant challenge on your agenda.

Assign Responsibilities for Above-the-Line Outcomes to the Individuals and Teams Required to Accomplish Them

With this step you complete your initial performance agenda. You know which challenges are being resourced and, equally important, you know which management discipline to use to achieve the goals in question. For those performance challenges that will apply the working group discipline, you should assign individuals their own SMART outcome-based goals, the sum of which at least equals the overall group challenge. For example, in the sales region story of this chapter, each of the 10 individual salespeople would have specific goals regarding revenue and new account growth, the sum of which ensured success against the region's overall goals.

For each goal demanding the team discipline, you must identify who on the team will be held mutually responsible for the SMART outcome-based goals in question. In most cases, the team members assigned will be a subset of your group. Occasionally, the team will be your entire group. Most often, however, success does not demand everyone to be on the team. Groups that specify "all" in the responsibility column for every team challenge are typically groups that really do not understand what the team discipline is about. For them, "all" means "none."

Sometimes you must invite one or more people who are *not* formally part of your group to join the team assigned to a particular outcome. Such was the case in the new account cycle time reduction challenge discussed earlier. In this case, the working arena required for success—the new account opening process—

extended beyond the sales region. If you, as sales region manager, had assigned responsibility for reducing the cycle time of this process to a team that comprised only your salespeople, they would rightly complain that the goal did not fit (see Chapter 5).

You might find yourself wondering how a sales region manager has the authority to assign team responsibility to people from accounting, distribution, and logistics (let alone separate manufacturing companies). The answer is simple: He or she doesn't! Still, if it is critical to the success of the restaurant supply company that the new account opening process be speeded up and better satisfy the needs of customers, then some team, some time, must take responsibility for results. The sales manager can initiate this effort through volunteering resources and, critically, making the challenge part of his or her region's performance agenda. If, notwithstanding that effort, no team gets formed or no team gels around the challenge, then the sales manager should move the challenge from above the line to below the line. The challenge itself remains an important priority, but it moves below the line because no current and sufficient resources are effectively assigned to it.

Monitor Performance and Make Adjustments

Performance agendas are critical management tools to help small groups set goals and priorities, and then choose when to use the working group and team disciplines to deliver results. *Every small group at every level of the organization should have a performance agenda in place*—and they should use their performance agendas to regularly review progress as well as make necessary adjustments. Whenever individuals or teams achieve the goals and outcomes above the line, then the group must decide what additional challenges to resource. Whenever new demands, challenges, strategies, programs, initiatives or other efforts crop up in the organization, small groups must review their performance agendas for completeness and prioritization. Finally, small groups must use performance agendas to keep a record of how they are coordinating with others throughout the organization. As already noted, it is the rare small group in today's challenging environment that does not have some outsiders listed as members of critical teams. By monitoring the progress of such teams, small groups effectively connect themselves to challenges that stretch beyond their formal responsibilities.

Exercise 8.1: Choose Your Discipline

Identify a handful of SMART outcome-based goals that your small group must deliver. With regard to each separate outcome, split yourselves into pairs and ask each pair to take 15 minutes to identify reasons for and against the working group discipline and for and against the team discipline. Gather as a full group and discuss the arguments. Then make a choice of which discipline makes the most sense for each outcome.

Exercise 8.2: Develop Common or Mutual Understanding

Gather a team that is responsible for a particular challenge. Ask the team to brainstorm and identify a variety of disagreements that exist about the team's purpose, goals, and working approach. You might also list disagreements regarding the interpretation of some analysis or situation the team faces. Pick any disagreement you want to start with. Ask people on the team to articulate their personal positions with regard to this disagreement. Discuss and debate among yourselves until each party to the disagreement can articulate to the other party's satisfaction that other party's point of view. Once you have achieved this level of mutual understanding, decide as a team how you will select a position and move on. Then go to the next disagreement on your list.

Exercise 8.3: Evaluate Team Progress

Use the questions in Figure 8.1 to determine how you are progressing as a team and what you might do to increase the odds of delivering the performance outcomes you seek to achieve.

Exercise 8.4: Put Together a Performance Agenda

Gather your small group together. Use the following steps to construct a performance agenda for your group:

- List the performance challenges confronting your small group.

- Convert each challenge into one or more SMART outcome-based goals that would indicate success.

- Determine which of these performance challenges and outcomes your group will staff and expect serious effort against.

- Draw a line between those challenges that are sufficiently resourced and those that are not.

- For challenges above the line, determine whether the outcomes indicated demand the working group or the team discipline.

- Assign responsibilities for above-the-line outcomes to the individuals and teams required to accomplish them. Remember to include people from other parts of your organization in teams when needed.

Exercise 8.5: Use Your Performance Agenda to Conduct an Operating Review of Your Small Group's Performance

At any time from two to five weeks following the creation of your performance agenda, gather your group and review progress against the challenges and outcomes in it. Remember to invite people from other parts of the organization if they are members of teams contributing to outcomes on your agenda. As you review progress, ask the relevant people:

- What is the status of this goal? Are we on track or not?

- What are the key opportunities and risks in achieving the outcomes?

- What lessons have you learned regarding the pursuit of this goal? What lessons have you learned about the management discipline involved?

- What modifications or additions, if any, would you make to the outcomes? To the choice of discipline and/or its application?

- What are the specific next steps needed to achieve this goal?

Organizationwide Performance

Vertical versus Horizontal Management Disciplines

Understanding the Two Disciplines for Organizationwide Performance

In Chapter 8, we explored the managerial disciplines required to achieve performance in a single small group. As mentioned there, the work of organizations ultimately breaks down into efforts by small groups and individuals. As you will recall, this same point is reflected in arena mapping (see Chapter 6), which disaggregates the work of organizations into the working arenas of single individuals and single teams (see the far right box of Figure 9.1). Our focus in Chapter 9 is to move from the righthand box of single individuals and single teams to the middle box and ask: What are the management disciplines that *combinations of multiple individuals and multiple teams* must use to deliver performance? We shift, then, from a focus on a single individual and single team to achieving organizationwide performance.

As you see in Figure 9.1, the three most common working arenas that demand organizationwide performance from combinations of individuals and teams are:

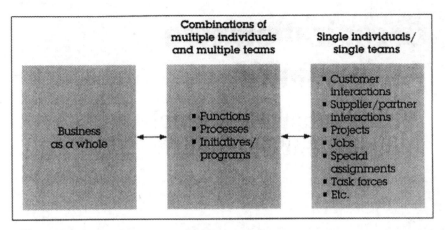

FIGURE 9.1 Working arenas for a single business.

- *Functions:* These are most familiar. They include classic business functions such as research and development, operations, distribution, marketing, sales, customer service, human resources, finance, and legal. In the classic pyramid model of organizations, functional performance is the sum of the performance of departments, which, in turn, are the sum of individual performances. In today's organizations, functional performance depends on the contributions of teams as well as individuals.

- *Processes:* These working arenas should also be familiar to you. Businesses have pursued process performance for nearly a decade now. Processes include *customer-driven processes* such as order generation through fulfillment, new product/service development, integrated logistics, and customer service, as well as *management processes* such as budgeting, planning, reviewing, hiring, training, career development, audit, and assessment. Process performance demands contributions from both individuals as well as teams.

- *Initiatives/programs:* No organization succeeds without using initiatives and programs to drive new ways of doing

things and delivering performance. Initiatives and programs, then, are about change. Chapter 10 discusses the
two management disciplines required to achieve both performance and change.

This chapter focuses on differentiating the *vertical/functional*
discipline required to deliver functional performance from the
horizontal/process discipline required to deliver process performance. Both demand that you apply the orientation we have
developed throughout this book. You must have SMART outcome-
based goals for the function or process in question. You must
work hard to put creative "both/and" tension into these goals and
to ensure that your goals matter to all the constituencies critical
to your organization's success. And you must subdivide the overall goals into SMART outcome-based goals for individuals and
teams.

The choice between vertical/functional and horizontal/
process disciplines depends on the performance outcomes you
wish to accomplish. With your SMART outcome-based goals in
hand, you and your colleagues must ask, "*Are we more likely to
achieve the desired organizationwide performance using the verti-
cal/functional discipline or the horizontal/process discipline?*"
Your answer should be:

- *Vertical/functional* when performance requires lots of individuals and teams to execute roughly *the same set of tasks*
  over and over again.

- *Horizontal/process* when performance requires lots of individuals and teams to execute *different tasks that must be
  connected and coordinated with one another.*

To quickly illustrate this, recall the example in Chapter 8 of the
restaurant supply company seeking to grow both revenues and
new accounts. This is a classic vertical/functional challenge. Success depends on lots of salespeople in sales regions throughout

the company executing the same family of tasks—namely, selling. Selling, of course, has many dimensions and challenges. Salespeople need to make sales calls to existing and potential customers, write up call reports, negotiate and close with customers, and communicate results to others in the company who must then follow up. Salespeople apply a rich variety of techniques and approaches to their tasks. But, notwithstanding all of the variation, the fact remains that salespeople throughout the company are executing the same family of tasks called selling. Organizationwide performance at growing both revenues and new accounts, therefore, demands the vertical/functional management discipline, with which you should be familiar:

- Set overall function goals.
- Divide overall function goals into subunit goals in which the number of subunits (departments, regions, etc.) reflects choices regarding span of control and span of communications.
- Further divide subunits if necessary.
- Assign individuals and/or teams responsibilities for goals.
- Ensure that individual/team, departmental, and functional goals are in alignment with overall organization performance direction and aspirations.
- Plan, budget, review, measure, and reward individual, department, and function performance.
- Design and deliver information, training, and career development support that reinforces functional excellence.

Recall that you, as the head of one sales region, decided to assemble a team from accounting, logistics, distribution, sales, and one or two manufacturers to recommend changes to increase the speed and customer satisfaction of opening new accounts. Assume that this team made a series of suggestions that were adopted by the president of the company. The question arises: Which management discipline is required to implement their recommendations?

The vertical/functional discipline will not work because the recommended changes require individuals and teams from sales, accounting, logistics, distribution, and, possibly, the supplying manufacturers to execute *different tasks in a well-connected and coordinated way.* Successful performance requires the horizontal/process discipline.

The horizontal/process discipline is far less familiar than the vertical/functional. The following Mindbook section explains the horizontal/process discipline in detail. First, however, we need to discuss the question of organization structure. Organization structure describes how work is formally divided up and assigned, and who reports to whom. Recall that Chapter 8 suggested that, when it comes a single small group, you worry less about organization structure and reporting relationships than about choosing when to use the working group discipline and when to use the team discipline. I recommended against debating whether you are a team or a working group because any single, small group should be flexible enough to shift from one discipline to another.

While single, small groups have such flexibility, whole organizations typically do not. When scores or hundreds of people must collaborate to achieve organizationwide performance, issues of structure and reporting relationships can be critical. Indeed, most organizations must choose which management discipline—vertical/functional or horizontal/process—they will need to use most often to achieve performance. And then they need to structure themselves accordingly. This is difficult, but, once again, it turns on performance. The question is this: *Does organizationwide performance today and in the future depend more on becoming continuously better at vertical/functional performance or continuously better at horizontal/process performance?*

The key words are "continuously better." Restructuring an organization and its reporting relationships demands a heavy investment of time and money. What you may not know (but it should make sense) is that people spend the vast majority of their time and effort doing the tasks assigned to them in their formal organization boxes. They also communicate far more with other people inside their silos than with people in other silos (i.e., other formal parts of the organization). As a result, in what is known as the *learning curve*, people become *continuously better* at the tasks formally assigned to them—tasks they perform repeatedly, and tasks they discuss with their organization neighbors.

Therefore, when organizations invest in restructuring formal task assignments and reporting relationships, the return on that investment depends on what the organization is seeking to have people become continuously better at doing. Look again at the example of the restaurant supply company. Should it formally structure itself vertically around functions or horizontally around processes?

The company should organize functionally around sales to meet the revenue and growth targets. Company success depends on people in sales becoming continuously better at selling. In contrast, improving the speed and customer satisfaction of new account opening demands that a variety of people from different parts of the company become continuously better at coordinating a series of different tasks. As a result, the restaurant supply company must seriously consider organizing around process, not function, if it wishes to excel at this performance challenge.

Increasingly, organization structures reflect hybrid combinations of functions and processes. Sometimes companies organize vertically in functions and sometimes horizontally in processes. At a minimum, many organizations have created *shadow* process structures that sit alongside the more dominant and longer-standing vertical/functional structures. A growing number of organizations have replaced some of their functions with formal process structures. However, I know of only a handful of organizations that have even considered, let alone transformed themselves into, the pure horizontal form.

The Horizontal/Process Discipline

It has been several years since I first coined the term *horizontal organization* and *Fortune* magazine hailed it as "the model for the next fifty years!" Over that period, I have observed many organizations grapple with performance challenges that demand the horizontal/process approach. There have been many lessons. Foremost among them is this: In choosing between the vertical/ functional and horizontal/process disciplines, you are choosing how to *connect work to performance not decision-making authority.* People who see this point—that the choice hinges on how best to do work—are people who succeed. In contrast, people who view the vertical versus horizontal choice primarily in terms of decision-making authority are people headed for trouble and disappointing performance outcomes.

As I have done throughout this book, I urge you to make your choice based on the performance outcomes you seek to achieve. Let's consider, then, the following example. You work for a large telephone company in a division that provides residential phone service. In the past few years, your division has taken a beating under deregulation. Now the new division head announces a vision and strategy for growing and retaining business from high-end residential customers. To succeed, your division must dramatically increase speed and customer satisfaction. You have been asked to join an effort with the goal of *ensuring that 100 percent of high-end residential customers, whether new or seeking upgrades or service changes, are fully set up within 24 hours of placing their orders and have zero billing defects.*

You and your colleagues decide that you must apply the horizontal/process discipline to this challenge. As you do, pay attention to the following basic principles for success.

Organize People and Work Primarily around Process Not Function

Your division of the telephone company must get continuously better at coordinating and connecting a variety of tasks that, up until now, have been organized functionally within sales, purchasing, inventory, warehousing, installation, supplier relations, billing, and customer service. Now you must organize these tasks and the people doing them around process, not function. To do so, map out the process by which work is done from the time of the customer order through full installation as well as accurate billing. Take whatever steps are needed to reengineer the process. Then, structure the work of your organization around the process itself.

Use Hierarchy to Link Work Flows and Subprocesses

Think for a moment about the value that hierarchy adds to organizations. Whenever organizations seek improved effectiveness and efficiency through the division of labor, hierarchy helps tie that divided labor back together again, particularly through setting direction, coordinating goals, and allocating scarce resources. Historically, hierarchy has been the most significant way to coordinate different functions. In the horizontal organization, the process itself is the primary coordinating device, not hierarchy. But hierarchy is still needed, especially if a single team cannot span the entire, end-to-end set of tasks required for the process in question.

Such is the case in the telephone company example. It would be difficult to assemble a small number of people from all the different functional disciplines and ask them, as a single team, to deliver end-to-end process performance. Instead, the full order through fulfillment process is likely to be subdivided into several subprocesses with teams or individuals assigned to deliver subprocess performance. As a result, you will need to appoint a hierarchically responsible person or team to oversee, direct, coordinate, and allocate scarce resources among the subprocess teams.

Push Ambiguity Up, Not Down

Do not confuse the horizontal organization with the matrix organization. In the matrix organization, ambiguity is pushed down the organization. If you are matrixed into two or three bosses, one with "solid line" and others with "dotted line" authority, then *you*—not your bosses—are responsible for figuring out how to optimize the different and competing directions. For example, in the telephone company case, imagine that you are the local department head for installation in a matrix organization. You get direction from sales about the importance of speed, from purchasing and inventory regarding cost and forecasting predictability, and from supplier relations with respect to equipment and service options. *You* are expected to integrate all these concerns, which, because they logically compete with one another, is difficult. In most matrix organizations, you would resolve this ambiguity in favor of whichever of your many bosses has the most power (the "solidest" line), as opposed to what's best for the customer.

In the horizontal organization, the responsibility for ambiguity is pushed up, not down. The difficult trade-offs among cost, predictability, speed, and supplier relations demand a whole-process perspective. That means the process owners (see below), not the people at the front lines, are primarily responsible for these tough, ambiguous challenges. And process owners resolve the ambiguity in favor of what's best for the customer at the end of the process.

Set and Monitor SMART End-of-Process Performance Goals That Benefit Customers, Shareholders, and the People of the Enterprise and Their Partners

Horizontal organization principles apply best to *customer-driven processes* such as order generation through fulfillment, new product or service development, customer service, and integrated logistics. You always find customers with real needs at the end of these processes. Through meeting customer needs, returns to shareholders and continued opportunities for people follow. You can use the cycle of sustainable performance to ensure that your end-of-process performance outcomes benefit all constituencies that matter (see Chapter 7). In the telephone case, such outcomes would include speed and service benefits for high-end residential customers; shareholder benefits with respect to market share, growth, and profitability; skills and opportunities for people of the enterprise with respect to the team and process disciplines as well as multiskilling in various technical and functional areas; and, possibly, alliance partner outcomes with respect to sales of equipment and service (e.g., long distance).

In specifying end-of-process performance outcomes, keep in mind the four yardsticks (Chapter 2) and "both/and" tension (Chapter 4). In fact, the overall goal in this example—*ensuring that 100 percent of high-end residential customers, whether new or seeking upgrades or service changes, are fully set up within 24 hours of placing their orders and have zero billing defects*—uses two of the four yardsticks (speed and on-expec performance) that are in creative tension with one another. You should avoid single-dimension, end-of-process performance outcomes that fail to demand creativity and trade-offs.

Assign Formal Ownership of Process and Process Performance

Today, most organizations appreciate the important contribution cross-functional work processes make to competitive success. Too many of these organizations, however, continue to resist assigning formal ownership and responsibility for process performance. If your company faces a performance challenge that demands continuous process improvement instead of continuous functional improvement, then you must name either an individual or a team as process owner, provide that individual or team with the resources needed to succeed, and hold the person or team responsible for process performance. If you do less than this, you will fail.

Make Teams the Principal Building Block of Performance

The team discipline reviewed in Chapter 8 combines multiple skills and perspectives against a common performance challenge. It is well-suited to process challenges because process performance demands coordination and connection among a variety of disciplines and activities. This does not mean that the individual or working group discipline is irrelevant. For example, it is conceivable that the telephone challenge might require that classic individual performance goals be assigned to customer service representatives taking customer orders over the phone. Still, when it comes to process performance, you will find that teams and the team discipline help to minimize the subdivision of work flows, minimize the use of hierarchy, and, most important, maximize end-of-process performance.

Combine Managerial and Nonmanagerial Activities As Often As Possible

As you move toward teams, you will have the option of making those teams self-managing. The more that teams do their own job design, scheduling, budgeting, hiring, peer evaluation, firing, goal setting, measurement, and cross-training, the more productive those teams become. Note well that teams must *learn* how to do these things effectively; you cannot simply designate teams as self-managing and expect them to adequately perform all these tasks. It takes time. But, the more effectively teams combine managerial and nonmanagerial activities, the more effectively they contribute to overall process performance.

Treat Multiple Skills and Competencies as the Rule, Not the Exception

The more skills that any single person can contribute to a process, the better. And the more people who can contribute multiple skills, the better. Indeed, a fundamental objective of organizing around process is to build multiple skills in people so that they can continuously improve how they work together to deliver process performance. As you pursue multiskilling, remember to pay attention to technical and functional skills, interpersonal and communication skills, problem-solving and decision-making skills, and the managerial skills and disciplines we are discussing throughout this book. Also note that the multiskilling objective of horizontal organizations starkly contrasts with the objective of vertical/functional organizations to have people become increasingly better at the same skill, not different ones.

Inform and Train People on a Just-in-Time-to-Perform Basis, Not on a Need-to-Know Basis

This management principle is not unique to the horizontal organization; it applies to all challenges whether vertical/functional, team, working group, or change-oriented. In a world where competitive advantage and sustained performance increasingly turn on how well organizations use information, information itself must be broadly, not narrowly, available. The habits and heritage of most established organizations are to use information for control and to make it available only on a need-to-know basis. Down that path lies failure. Instead, you must make information available on a need-to-perform basis.

Similarly, you need to design and deliver training and learning opportunities to people on a just-in-time-to-perform basis. That means, for example, that people should be required to bring SMART outcome-based goals to training and education sessions. And those responsible for training and education should set and achieve goals that refer explicitly to the kind of outcomes they are training people to accomplish (refer to the hybrid goals discussed in Chapter 5). Far too many organizations offer training at the convenience of the trainer and without any required performance outcomes from those trained. The poor return on training dollars speaks for itself.

Maximize Supplier and Customer Contact

Customer-driven processes, by definition, have customers at the end. Many of them also have key suppliers associated with them. It stands to reason, then, that the more you integrate supplier and customer contact, the better you will perform. The more that people who are doing the work of a process interact with customers, the better they understand and respond to customer needs. The more they interact with suppliers, the better they coordinate and innovate in service of mutual customers.

Use Technology and Management Processes to Maintain Functional Excellence

An immediate objection to the horizontal organization concerns functional excellence. After decades of building functional expertise through vertical/functional organization, people question whether the benefits of cross-functional coordination outweigh the risk of diminishing or deteriorating functional expertise. This is a fair concern. The primary answer, of course, lies in responding to the key question about performance asked at the beginning of this chapter: Does organizationwide performance turn more on continuous improvement at the same set of vertical/functional tasks or continuous improvement at connecting and coordinating across different horizontal/process tasks?

Even if your answer emphasizes process over function, you do not have to abandon functional excellence. You certainly should do nothing to intentionally destroy it. You can use technology to robustly connect people with similar functional interests and concerns—and you can create centers of excellence or centers of competence to manage careers, provide training, assemble regular discussion forums, and conduct functional learning projects, all as means to retaining cutting-edge functional expertise.

Reward Individual Skill Development and Team and Process Performance, Not Just Individual Performance

Organizations cannot achieve maximum process performance if all the rewards and recognition are based solely on individual performance goals. A quick reread of these principles of horizontal design indicates why. Optimal and continuous process performance depends on multiskilling; therefore, you must recognize and reward individual skill development. Process performance depends on teams; therefore, you must recognize and reward team performance. Process performance itself must also be rewarded. In the telephone example, all those who work hard to ensure that 100 percent of high-end residential customers are fully set up within 24 hours of placing their orders without any billing defects should be recognized and rewarded for their success.

Exercise 9.1: Choose Your Discipline

Consider a performance challenge facing your business or shared service unit. Use the exercises in Chapters 1 through 4 to articulate one or more SMART outcome-based goals that would indicate success at this challenge. Ask yourselves whether you are more likely to achieve these performance goals using the vertical/functional discipline or the horizontal/process discipline. Remember to favor the vertical/functional discipline if performance depends on lots of individuals and teams executing roughly *the same set of tasks* over and over again. In contrast, favor the horizontal/process discipline if performance depends on lots of individuals and teams executing *different tasks that must be connected and coordinated with one another.* Split into pairs and take up to 30 minutes to develop pro and con arguments for each discipline. Then gather as a whole group and review these arguments. Remember to base your arguments on the specific performance goals you have set and how best to achieve them.

Exercise 9.2: Profile Your Effectiveness at Using the Vertical/Functional Discipline to Deliver Performance

Pick an organizationwide performance challenge and a set of goals that you have chosen to achieve using the vertical/functional discipline. Remember that success demands that you:

- Set overall function goals.
- Divide overall function goals into subunit goals in which the number of subunits (departments, regions, etc.) reflects choices regarding span of control and span of communications.
- Further divide subunits if necessary.

- Assign individuals and/or teams responsibilities for goals.

- Ensure that individual/team, departmental, and functional goals are in alignment with overall organization performance direction and aspirations.

- Plan, budget, review, measure, and reward individual, department, and function performance.

- Design and deliver information, training, and career development support that reinforces functional excellence.

Accordingly, gather together any set of colleagues involved in achieving this challenge, and discuss how effectively you are progressing against the challenge and toward the desired outcomes. Use the following chart to profile your effectiveness, and then to identify and agree upon steps you can take to accelerate and improve the odds of success.

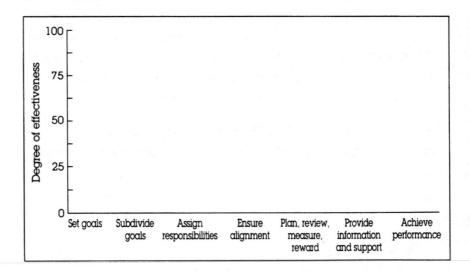

Exercise 9.3: Must You Reorganize?

Gather the leaders of your business or shared service unit. Spend the time necessary to lay out each major challenge facing you. For each challenge, use Exercise 9.1 to identify whether the vertical/functional discipline or the horizontal/process discipline makes the most sense. Once you have the complete picture before you, discuss among yourselves whether and how you might need to reorganize the formal responsibilities and tasks of your business or shared service unit. Remember that the key issue is whether and to what extent your business or shared service unit depends on people becoming continuously better at vertical/functional performance or at horizontal/process performance. You may find that you will need to use a mixed set of functions and processes to deliver overall organization performance. Discuss among yourselves how best to do so, including how and when to use formal functions and processes, shadow functions and processes, and centers of excellence and competency. Finally, remember to avoid using a matrix approach that pushes ambiguity down instead of up.

Exercise 9.4: Profile Your Effectiveness at Using the Horizontal/Process Discipline to Deliver End-of-Process Performance

Pick an organizationwide performance challenge and a set of goals that you have chosen to achieve using the horizontal/ process discipline. Remember that success demands that you:

- Organize people and work primarily around process not function.

- Use hierarchy to link work flows and subprocesses.

- Push ambiguity up, not down.

- Set and monitor SMART end-of-process performance goals that benefit customers, shareholders, and the people of the enterprise and their partners.

- Assign formal ownership of process and process performance.

- Make teams the principal building block of performance.

- Combine managerial and nonmanagerial activities as often as possible.

■ Treat multiple skills and competencies as the rule, not the exception.

■ Inform and train people on a just-in-time-to-perform basis, not on a need-to-know basis.

■ Maximize supplier and customer contact.

■ Use technology and management processes to maintain functional excellence.

■ Reward individual skill development and team and process performance, not just individual performance.

Gather any group of colleagues participating in meeting this performance challenge, and discuss how effectively you are progressing against the challenge and outcomes at hand. Use the following chart to profile your effectiveness, and then to identify and agree upon steps you can take to accelerate and improve the odds of success.

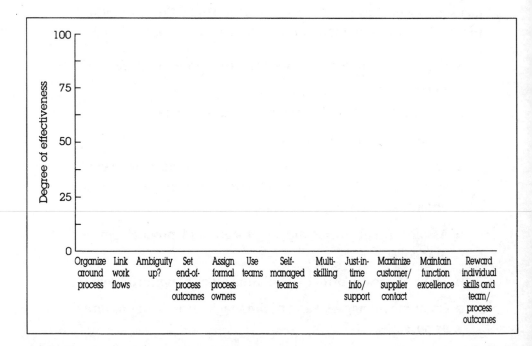

CHAPTER 10

Performance and Change

Decision-Driven versus Behavior-Driven Management Disciplines

Understanding the Two Disciplines
for Achieving Success in the Face of Change

We live in an age of change. Organizations that once profited through caution now routinely fail when their people ignore or defer change. And yet, it is human nature to find change difficult, especially if change dares people to alter that which is most fundamental—their behaviors, their skills, and their relationships with others. In *Taking Charge of Change,* I noted that the most difficult task confronting any organization today is to achieve new levels of performance that depend on specific behavioral, skill, and working relationship changes among lots of people who already work in the organization. In contrast, organizations succeed more often in the face of changes that, while requiring new decisions and directions, build on instead of belie what their people already know how to do well.

Study after study shows that up to four out of five change efforts either fail or seriously suboptimize. Looking behind these numbers, I discovered that most of the successes involved change that demanded tough decisions but little fundamental or widespread behavioral shifts. In *Taking Charge of Change,* I called this *performance only* change. Most of the failures concerned the more difficult challenge of both performance and fundamental behavioral change—what I called *performance and change.* Since writing *Taking Charge of Change,* I have found that people learn and remember this critical distinction better when I use the terms *decision-driven* change (instead of "performance only") and *behavior-driven* change (instead of "performance and change"); therefore, I will use these labels in this book.

In decision-driven change, the organization faces important changes. The changes themselves might reflect strategies or market or product opportunities, mergers, acquisitions, outsourcing, reengineering, strategic alliances, refinancings, and so on. Indeed, there is no limit to the kind of challenges that might be decision-driven. In decision-driven change, leaders must make tough decisions, communicate them well, and get people's buy-in and commitment. But what makes any particular change decision-driven is the fact that there are enough people in the organization who *already have the needed skills, behaviors, and working relationships to implement the new decisions and directions.*

Leaders must also create, communicate, and obtain buy-in to tough new decisions in behavior-driven change. Again, the changes might include any number of challenges currently facing organizations, such as new strategies, markets, alliances, or technologies. What makes any particular change behavior-driven instead of decision-driven, however, is the fact that the leaders' decisions, no matter how well made, communicated, or bought-into, are not enough. In behavior-driven change, *a critical mass of people in the organization must learn specific new skills, behaviors, and working relationships to implement the new decisions and directions.* As *Taking Charge of Change* discussed at length and this chapter summarizes, the managerial discipline demanded by behavior-driven change differs from the discipline required to achieve decision-driven change.

The high failure rate of change efforts in organizations primarily occurs because leaders, executives, managers, and others apply the well-known and longer practiced decision-driven managerial discipline to behavior-driven change challenges. We have discussed this kind of square peg, round hole mismatch before in this book. Analogous failures occur when small groups apply the working group discipline to team performance challenges or vice versa (see Chapter 8), and when organizations apply the vertical/functional discipline to horizontal/process performance challenges or vice versa (see Chapter 9). Don't make this mistake. Pay attention to the critical distinction between decision-driven change and behavior-driven change and, as always, let performance outcomes be your guide.

Imagine, then, that your organization faces some significant and particular change. You and your colleagues ask yourselves, "What would be the SMART outcomes if we succeeded in mastering this change?" With those goals in mind, you must then ask yourselves whether success depends on yes or no answers to the following four questions:

1. Does all or any significant part of our organization have to become very good at one or more things that we are not good at today?

2. Do lots of already employed people have to change specific skills, behaviors, and/or working relationships?

3. Does our organization have a positive record of success with changes of this type?

4. Do those people who must implement the new decisions and directions understand what they need to do and urgently believe the time to act is now?

If you answer no to the first two questions and yes to the second two, then you can deliver the SMART outcomes through decision-driven change. You can rely on the existing skills, competencies, working relationships, self-confidence, and motivation of the people in your organization to implement the new decisions and to achieve the new goals. If, however, you answer yes to the first two questions and no to the second two, then you face behavior-driven change.

Figure 10.1 provides a series of indicators to help you determine whether you face decision-driven or behavior-driven change. *No organizational challenge is as difficult as behavior-driven change.* Consequently, if you can find a way to achieve success through the decision-driven approach, you should pursue it. Many challenges that seem at first to be behavior-driven can, on further analysis, turn out to be decision-driven.

Consider the following example. You work at LincolnBooks and the 1990s have not been kind to your company. Coming into the decade, you were neck and neck with Barnes & Noble in branded retail book distribution. Then, regrettably, you and your colleagues turned your backs on change. Now, as the decade closes, Barnes & Noble has gained huge share through its super-stores, and both Barnes & Noble and Amazon.com have taken big, early leads in eCommerce. Both Barnes & Noble and Amazon.com have significant leverage over publishers, giving each competitive advantages with respect to cost, speed, and availability. At long last, you and other leaders at LincolnBooks decide to act by undertaking three critical initiatives:

- You create two new divisions—LincolnKids and Lincoln-Grads—to focus on the children's and college markets.

- You establish LincolnWeb to compete in eCommerce.

- You seek a series of exclusive arrangements with publishers to provide LincolnBooks with sole distribution rights to new authors for limited periods in exchange for certain volume commitments.

It is possible that each of these three initiatives is decision-driven. The creation of the two new divisions is definitely decision-driven. People at LincolnBooks have the skills, behaviors, and

Question/issue	Decision-driven indicator	Behavior-driven indicator
1. Does all or any significant part of our organization have to get very good at one or more things that we are not good at today?	No	Yes
How clear is the link between performance results and the capabilities the organization must get good at?	Very clear	Not so clear
Just how new and how different is this challenge?	Not so new or different	Very new and very different
How many new capabilities must the organization master?	None or one	Several
How much time does the organization have to learn the new capabilities?	Lots of time	Not much time
2. Do lots of already employed people have to change specific skills, behaviors, and/or working relationships?	No	Yes
Can you change assets or policies instead of people?	Yes	No
Can you redirect the efforts of enough already capable people?	Yes	No
Can you hire enough new people instead of changing skills and behaviors of existing people?	Yes	No
How many existing people must learn new skills and behaviors?	Few/not many	Lots and lots
How much will people have to collaborate across organizational boundaries?	Not much	Often and a lot
3. Does our organization have a positive record of success with changes of this type?	Yes	No
Has your organization successfully tackled something like this before?	Yes	No
Are there any? many? people in your organization who have succeeded at this type of challenge, whether in your company or others?	Lots	Few
4. Do those people who must implement the new decisions and directions understand what they need to do and urgently believe the time to act is now?	Yes	No
How many people in relevant jobs understand the need for change?	Enough people in the relevant jobs	Few people in the relevant jobs

(continued)

FIGURE 10.1 Do you face decision-driven or behavior-driven change?

Question/issue	Decision-driven indicator	Behavior-driven indicator
How many people in relevant jobs can articulate the link between the change at hand and the performance outcomes required?	Enough	Few/none
How many people in relevant jobs can articulate the implications of the change challenge for how they do their work?	Enough	Few/none
How many people in relevant jobs feel emotionally compelled and desirous of making the changes at hand?	Enough	Few/none
How many people in relevant jobs have made plans or taken action to move forward with the changes at hand?	Enough	Few/none
What kind of reinforcement can people expect from the existing organizational structure, reporting relationships, and reward and recognition approaches?	Lots/positive	Little/negative

FIGURE 10.1 *Continued.*

working relationships needed to extend the LincolnBooks brand in the manner indicated. Yes, those working in the new divisions will have a new and different focus, but no one needs to learn anything fundamentally different about the book business or about how to relate to coworkers, customers, or others.

Whether the eCommerce initiative is decision-driven or behavior-driven depends entirely on how you think about the second of the four questions mentioned earlier. If you and your colleagues choose to ask people currently employed at Lincoln-Books to learn all the skills, behaviors, and working relationships needed to succeed on the World Wide Web, then they will face behavior-driven change. However, if you go out and hire new people with eCommerce experience, then the chances are that you can succeed here in decision-driven fashion. True, some (but not a lot) of the existing LincolnBooks people might have to shift over to the web business, but their numbers could be relatively small, and they would have expert guidance and direction from the newcomers.

Finally, the new authors initiative also might turn out to be decision-driven, particularly if the deals cut with publishers can be executed through LincolnBooks' existing skills. LincolnBooks either already has people with the skills and publishing relationships to make these deals or it can easily hire the few needed. If, on the other hand, people throughout LincolnBooks' supply chain, and particularly the managers and others in the retail stores, would need to learn specific new skills, behaviors, or working relationships to make the new authors effort a success, then you might face behavior-driven change. That, however, is unlikely.

The decision-driven managerial discipline should be familiar. That does not mean it is easy or guaranteed to produce results. To apply it well, you must:

- *Make performance-oriented, fact-based decisions.* Decision-driven change starts with decisions. Leaders who pursue endless preparatory discussions, analyses, and deliberations fail. Moreover, decisions must be fact-based; otherwise, leaders find it hard to communicate a clear vision about what has to change and why. Finally, decisions must link tightly to performance. If leaders cannot articulate the specific performance outcomes they seek through the decisions they make, they and others won't be able to translate decisions into meaningful action.

- *Ground decisions and directions in strategy.* Leaders must support their decisions with a compelling and pressing case for change, and that, in turn, requires that decisions be firmly grounded in strategy. No decision, no matter how well made or communicated, will produce the desired performance if the decision reflects a flawed strategy. Leaders must understand and master the strategic context, which, in today's world, means classic concerns for competitors, suppliers, distribution channels, customers, and other relevant third parties such as regulators in addition to newer considerations such as strategic alliances, core competencies, and technology.

- *Align your organization in support of your decisions.* Organizational arrangements must make sense in light of the decisions leaders make. You cannot expect to produce performance results and outcomes that differ from those the organization is set up to pursue. In this respect, it is often a good idea to shift responsibilities among top managers in order to better accomplish the decision-driven change at hand. Remember, however, that organizational alignment can also involve more than top management shifts. As discussed at length in Chapters 5 through 7, leaders need to be sure which working arenas are most critical to any given decision and how those arenas are aligned to meet the needs of customers, shareholders, and the people of the enterprise.

- *Develop a clear vision of what has to change and why.* Effective visions of what has to change and why are simple. They contain a small number of clear, easily remembered aspirations. As mentioned, they are sound (grounded in facts and strategy) and purposeful (linked tightly to performance that matters to customers, shareholders, and the people of the enterprise). Finally, they are both meaningful (they give all affected people a strong sense of what *they* must do) and inclusive (they offer an exciting future to all who must participate).

- *Communicate, communicate, communicate.* Leaders can never overcommunicate. They cannot spend too much time with too many different groups too often. Moreover, leaders must understand and practice both parts of effective communication: Tell the truth and listen. Finally, leaders must remember to communicate to all the people who matter, including customers, shareholders (and their proxies), partners, and, of course, the people of the enterprise.

- *Gain buy-in from relevant people and groups.* Leaders will know they have buy-in from relevant people and groups when they are certain that those people understand and can articulate the implications of the change at hand, clearly see the link between the change and the performance outcomes sought, know what actions to take, and are taking those actions. Buy-in, then, is about understanding *and* action—not just understanding alone.

- *Stay focused on performance outcomes and results.* Leaders must remain maniacally focused on performance outcomes and results that matter to customers, shareholders, and the people of the enterprise. Doing so demands that leaders learn and use all of the tools and techniques we have discussed in this book. Only by concentrating on performance can leaders assure themselves and those they lead that the decisions that sparked the change continue to make sense and, most important, continue to make a difference.

Managing Behavior-Driven Change

Assume that you face behavior-driven change. Perhaps your organization is tackling a total quality initiative for the first time (or for a second or third time, having failed in the past). Maybe your company is undertaking a new strategy that depends on developing one or more new core competencies such as becoming customer-driven. Possibly you are reengineering in some profound and novel way. Or, it could be that performance and success now depend on numbers of already employed people throughout your organization learning some of the managerial disciplines that we have reviewed in this book, including the performance discipline, the team discipline, and/or the horizontal/process discipline.

Whatever the change, you and your colleagues have determined that success depends on lots of already employed people learning specific new behaviors, skills, and working relationships. As you contemplate what lies ahead, remember this: *Leaders must still make and communicate decisions that are fact-based, strategically sound, adequately linked to performance, and well communicated and bought into.*

Decisions, however, are not enough. Instead, both the decisions and the performance outcomes sought depend on people in your organization learning specific new skills, behaviors, and relationships. That challenge, in turn, is characterized by a hard, unalterable, and timeless truth: *Only adults can take responsibility for their own behavior change.*

Recall your overweight, stressed-out friend from Chapter 2. No matter how supportive and helpful you and others might be, the fact remains that only your friend can take responsibility for making the eating and exercise changes demanded by his aspirations to lose weight and feel better. Whether he takes that responsibility depends on a variety of factors contained in the *wheel of personal change* (see Figure 10.2). Each part of this wheel represents a potential source of anxiety, reluctance, or resistance. If you seek to understand and help your friend—or if you seek to understand and help anyone in your organization—to take personal responsibility for behavior change, then figure out which parts of the wheel are most troublesome and how best to respond.

The essence of behavior-driven change is personal responsibility. If you face behavior-driven change in your organization, you must work hard to continually increase the number of people taking personal responsibility for their own change. Figure 10.3 illustrates this challenge and contrasts it with decision-driven change. In the decision-driven curve, you can rely on well-made and well-communicated decisions to quickly reach the people who must set and achieve goals. This approach to behavior-driven change, however, fails because leaders confuse wide-

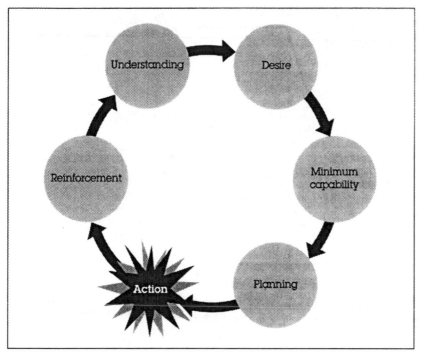

FIGURE 10.2 Wheel of personal change.

spread and well-communicated decisions with widespread personal responsibility for change. When leaders use decision-
driven approaches to manage behavior-driven change, they soon
see rapid deterioration in the number of people effectively contributing (see middle curve in Figure 10.3). The best path to successful behavior-driven change is one that slowly and surely
builds an increasing number of people taking personal responsibility for making both performance and change happen (see the
behavior-driven curve in Figure 10.3).

Success demands that you apply the 10 principles in the
behavior-driven management discipline.

1. *Keep performance, not change, the primary objective of
   behavior and skill change.*   The vast majority of people in
   organizations resist behavior and skill change if they
   believe it is an exercise in futility. If you cannot effectively

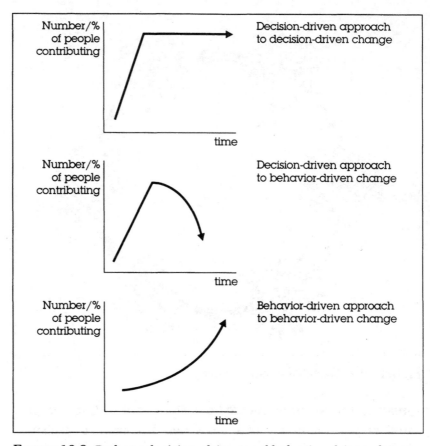

FIGURE 10.3 Paths to decision-driven and behavior-driven change.

link specific performance outcomes to the change you ask people to make, then you are likely to see change only among the small group of early adopters and change seekers who typically number no more than 5 to 10 percent of any organization. With respect to any initiative, program, training effort, or other activity, you must insist on asking, "Why are we doing this?" Your answer must point to one or more SMART outcome-based performance goals that matter to customers, shareholders, and the people who must change. Otherwise, you will slip into the trap of change for its own sake.

2. *Focus on continually increasing the number of people taking responsibility for their own performance and change.* Use the wheel of personal change to understand why people are anxious and reluctant to take personal responsibility for change. Most important, work hard to get people to take action in a performance context that matters (which is why *action* is stressed in Figure 10.2). Employ the tools and techniques of Chapters 1 through 5 to help people craft and commit to SMART outcome-based performance goals that they can accomplish only by taking personal responsibility for some underlying skill or behavior change.

Remember this: Do not ask people to commit to change; ask them to commit to performance. For example, do not ask people to commit to being a team; instead, ask them to commit to a performance outcome that demands the team discipline. Do not ask people to commit to quality; ask them to commit to specific speed and customer satisfaction goals that demand the application of total quality management disciplines. Do not ask people to commit to creating the best place to work; ask them to commit to specific performance outcomes that can be accomplished only through practicing the kind of values and behaviors associated with best places to work.

There are four basic strategies you can use to gain personal performance commitments from people: (1) voluntarism, (2) hierarchy, (3) teams, and (4) exchange. In the first, people *voluntarily* commit themselves to the change at hand. You want to ensure that along with their enthusiasm for change comes a commitment to specific outcome-based goals that will make a difference. Second, if you are the direct boss over people, then you can use *hierarchy* to demand that they commit themselves to an outcome-based goal relevant to the change. You can also use hierarchy when you are not the direct boss, but its effectiveness often deteriorates in the face of organization realities.

Third, you can *team* up with others in pursuit of performance, much as the sales region manager did in Chapter 9 in the restaurant supply story about improving the new account opening process. Fourth, you can make opportunities and resources that you control available to others only on condition that, in *exchange,* they commit to specific outcome-based goals that matter to the change challenge before you.

3. *Ensure that each person always knows why his or her performance and change matter to the purpose and results of the whole organization.* The worst nightmare of anyone facing personal responsibility for behavior change is not knowing why it matters or what difference it might make. In today's world, jobs are livelihoods and organizations are communities. When change threatens a person's job, it puts at risk housing, insurance, friendships, and even a person's sense of identity and purpose. People are more likely to constructively focus these anxieties if they know what specific performance outcomes they can achieve and how these outcomes matter to the organization. Moreover, do not fool yourself that gathering people together at the beginning of a change initiative and effectively communicating why each person's contribution matters is enough. As a leader of behavior-driven change, you must make sure that *every person* understands why his or her performance and change matter *every day.*

4. *Put people in a position to learn by doing and provide them with the information and support needed just in time to perform.* Nothing is more critical to change than learning. As indicated by the starburst element labeled "Action" in the wheel of personal change depicted in Figure 10.2, adults learn best when they apply new behaviors, skills, and relationships in a real performance context that matters. In contrast, studies have shown that, within one to

two weeks, adults forget over 90 percent of what they learned in training programs unconnected to any actual performance challenge or context. People facing behavior change do need information, training, and education support. To best help them, you should concentrate most of that support on the people who have made personal commitments to SMART outcome-based performance goals that matter to the challenge at hand.

5. *Embrace improvisation.* So long as people are pursuing performance outcomes that matter to the change being faced, give them plenty of room for experimentation. People succeed with new behavior, skills, and relationships by self-discovering what works and what doesn't. That means they must have the chance to learn through success as well as failure. Moreover, if people throughout your organization must learn new ways of working, logic suggests that no one—including you—has figured out the single best path.

6. *Use team performance to drive change whenever demanded.* The team discipline provides the single most powerful vehicle for succeeding at behavior-driven change. Teams provide the performance focus and the personal reinforcement and support so critical during periods of behavior-driven change. In fact, in my experience and observation, I have never heard of any real team whose members did not learn something valuable from their successful performance as a team. But remember this: The team discipline works only when small groups have performance goals that demand the real-time integration of multiple skills and perspectives. Therefore, use the team discipline as often as performance goals allow you to do so. Do not, however, put people in teams merely for the sake of having teams.

7. *Concentrate organization designs on the work people do, not the decision-making authority they have.* Adults learn

new skills, behaviors, and working relationships best in the context of real work that is connected to real performance outcomes that matter. Thus, if you and your colleagues need to redesign how people do real work in your organization, go ahead and do so. You will find the discussion in Chapter 9 particularly helpful. Do not, however, confuse the redesign of real work with the rearrangement of top management decision-making authority. It often makes sense to realign decision-making authority in decision-driven change. However, you will find it largely a waste of precious time and energy to reorganize decision-making authority (particularly near the top of the organization) as a prelude to behavior-driven change. While you argue over political turf, the majority of people who must take personal responsibility for performance and change will simply adopt a wait-and-see attitude.

8. *Create and focus energy and meaningful language.* The two scarcest resources during a period of behavior-driven change are energy and meaningful language; whereas, the two scarcest resources during a period of decision-driven change are money and talent. Effective leaders of behavior-driven change create and focus energy by challenging people to make personal commitments to performance and change and then providing just-in-time support to help those people learn, perform, and succeed. Effective leaders also create and focus energy by ensuring that all concurrent change initiatives, whether decision-driven or behavior-driven, are harmonized (see principle no. 9). Finally, behavior-driven change leaders work hard to find the most meaningful words, themes, and phrases that can provide inspiration, confidence, and real learning. When people speak about their work and performance in fundamentally new and different ways, they also work and perform in new ways. In my experience, every organization

that has succeeded with behavior-driven change has coined significant and meaningful pieces of new language in the process.

9. *Harmonize and integrate the change initiatives in your organization, including those that are decision-driven as well as behavior-driven.* This principle asks you to align initiatives, not management structures. Unlike the organizational alignment challenge of decision-driven change, which seeks to find the best *static* picture of decision-making authority, this principle demands that you make rational sense out of a *dynamic* picture of change efforts and initiatives. For example, return to the story of USProducts introduced in Chapter 7. You will recall that the company had undertaken a variety of initiatives, including some that were decision-driven (global expansion, 20/20 financial performance, and talent imperative) and some that were behavior-driven (reengineering, total customer satisfaction, and teams). To this mix, the CEO was considering adding three new initiatives: a merger, a strategic alliance, and downsizing. From my perspective, having six concurrent initiatives was already pushing the limits of any organization's capacity to absorb change. As we discussed, adding an initiative such as downsizing to this particular mix would disrupt whatever harmonization existed and destroy (not create) the energy needed.

10. *Practice leadership based on the courage to live the change you wish to bring about.* The golden rule of leading behavior-driven change is to "do unto yourself what you would have others do unto themselves." The only person for whom you can take responsibility is yourself. People faced with behavior-driven change follow leaders who put themselves at risk and who have the courage to commit themselves to performance goals that demand new skills, behaviors, and working relationships. On the other hand,

leaders who do not challenge themselves to take the risks they are asking of others typically inspire caution, not action. Leaders of behavior-driven change, then, must confront how their own behavior and performance must change if they hope to lead others to do the same.

WORKBOOK

Exercise 10.1: Do You Face Decision-Driven or Behavior-Driven Change?

Together with a group of colleagues, identify a challenge currently confronting your organization. Take time to create illustrative performance outcomes that would indicate success for this challenge, using exercises from Chapters 1 through 4. With the challenge and outcomes in mind, use the following four questions to determine whether you face decision-driven or behavior-driven change. Ask yourselves the following questions: "In order for us to succeed at this challenge and deliver these performance outcomes . . .

1. Does all or any significant part of our organization have to become very good at one or more things that we are not good at today?

2. Do lots of already employed people have to change specific skills, behaviors, and/or working relationships?

3. Does our organization have a positive record of success with changes of this type?

4. Do those people who must implement the new decisions and directions understand what they need to do and urgently believe the time to act is now?

Use Figure 10.1 to enrich your discussion.

Exercise 10.2: Can You Make the Change Decision-Driven?

Consider any change challenge in front of you that you believe is behavior-driven. Together with a group of colleagues, use the questions asked in Figure 10.1 to attempt to find ways to make the challenge into a decision-driven change. For example, you might be able to hire enough new people or shift the focus to changing assets or non-behavior-dependent policies. Maybe you can back-burner this change to give you a lot more time. Or maybe you can find enough people in your enterprise who have met this challenge in previous jobs and companies.

Exercise 10.3: Profile the Effectiveness of Your Decision-Driven Change Effort

Gather a group of colleagues and take the time needed to determine how effectively your decision-driven change effort is proceeding. Discuss among yourselves each of the key aspects of managing decision-driven change, including the following:

- Make performance-oriented, fact-based decisions.

- Ground decisions and directions in strategy.

- Align your organization in support of your decisions.

- Develop a clear vision of what has to change and why.

- Communicate, communicate, communicate.

- Gain buy-in from relevant people and groups.

- Stay focused on performance outcomes and results.

Use the following chart to profile how effectively you are managing the decision-driven change effort. Discuss and agree among yourselves on the steps you can take to improve your likelihood of success at delivering performance.

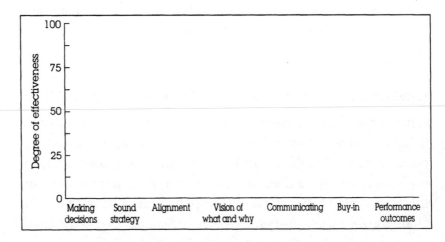

Exercise 10.4: Specify the "From/To's" of Behavior-Driven Change

If you believe some particular performance challenge requires behavior-driven change, take time to articulate the specific changes needed for each category of people and roles affected by the challenge. Use the following template to guide your efforts.

Performance challenge: _____

People/roles affected: _____

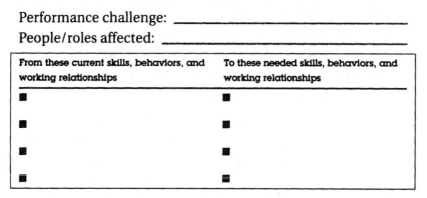

From these current skills, behaviors, and working relationships	To these needed skills, behaviors, and working relationships
■	■
■	■
■	■
■	■

You should also articulate those existing skills, behaviors, and working relationships that do not need to change, yet remain critical to success. Gather together anyone who joins you in facing the change. If the group becomes very large, use breakout groups to manage people's input and participation effectively.

Exercise 10.5: Develop a Behavior-Driven Change Strategy

Consider some particular behavior-driven change challenge facing your organization. Recall that the key to succeeding is gaining personal performance and change commitments from an increasing number of relevant people. There are only four ways to gain such commitments from people in organizations: (1) voluntarism, (2) hierarchy, (3) teams, and (4) exchange. Therefore, gather other leaders of this change effort and take a day or two to discuss and agree upon the following:

■ What SMART outcome-based goals would indicate success for your organization in this change effort? (Use selected exercises from Chapters 1 through 4.)

- What are the working arenas and who are the people most critical to success? (Use selected exercises from Chapters 5 and 6.)

- What are some illustrative SMART outcome-based goals to which you would like to see people in the relevant working arenas commit? How do those goals coordinate and align with one another? (Use exercises from Chapters 1 through 6.)

- As you consider the people most critical to this change effort, what are the specific new skills, behaviors, and working relationships they must master to succeed at delivering performance? (Use Exercise 10.4.)

- What are the sources of readiness and reluctance among the people who face behavior-driven change? (Use the wheel of personal change in Figure 10.2 to guide your discussion.)

- Who among the relevant people will you initially target to gain personal commitments to outcomes that matter? Why these people?

- What are some illustrative SMART outcome-based goals you would like these targeted people to commit to? Why do you believe they can achieve these goals only if they take personal responsibility for the kind of skill, behavior, and working relationship changes articulated earlier?

- What tactics will you use to gain goal commitments from the targeted people: voluntarism? hierarchy? team? exchange?

- How will you ensure that the tactics you select have the optimum chance of succeeding?

Remember that, in addition to developing these aspects of your strategy, you must also ensure that the required decisions are made and communicated. Use Exercise 10.3 to guide this aspect of your discussion.

CHAPTER 11

Putting It All Together

Manage Your Organization for Performance

Build an Outcomes Management System in Your Company

You can deploy the concepts, frameworks, tools, and techniques of this book to establish an outcomes management system in your organization. Your objective is performance. You seek to establish a system and set of practices to help the people of your enterprise routinely set and update the SMART outcome-based goals that matter most to success as well as to choose which management disciplines to use to achieve their goals. The outcomes management system will enable everyone to see how the goals in your organization fit together and make sense from a variety of critical perspectives, including:

- *Top management/whole organization.* From a top management perspective, you will see how all the goals of your organization make sense in light of the your company's vision, strategy, and performance challenges. You will see the big picture of what your organization is seeking to achieve, and how each and every working arena and subgoal contributes to results that matter to customers, to shareholders, and to the people of your enterprise and their partners.

- *Each person:* Every individual in your organization will have a set of SMART outcome-based goals that he or she is pursuing; will understand how and why their goals contribute to customers, shareholders, and themselves; will see how their goals logically reinforce the larger directions and strategies of the organization; will know which management disciplines make the most sense to use; and will see the link between their goals and the rewards, recognition, opportunities, and skills they hope to attain.

- *Each small group:* Every small group will have a focused and updated performance agenda (see Chapter 8) that specifies the outcomes the group is pursuing and the choice of either team or working group discipline for success. Each small group will also see how its outcomes align and coordinate with the goals of other working arenas and the organization as a whole.

- *Each working arena:* From the perspective of any working arena in the organization, you will quickly grasp how the SMART outcome-based goals for that arena contribute to the success of other working arenas and the organization as a whole; how smaller working arenas such as groups and individuals help achieve the goals of the larger arena; how the goals of that arena make sense in terms of customers, shareholders, and the people of the enterprise and the most critical performance challenges facing the organization; which management disciplines make the most sense to use for success; and how the formal and informal organization of the company can and should be adjusted, if at all.

- *Each performance challenge:* You will see how the SMART outcomes that need to be achieved by the relevant working arenas for any single performance challenge coordinate and align with one another, and how the goals for different performance challenges make sense and fit together.

- *Each critical constituency that matters:* Regardless of the scope of the working arena in question—the whole organization, business units, shared services, initiatives, functions, processes, small groups, individuals—you will see how the outcomes pursued matter to customers, shareholders, and the people of your enterprise and their partners. The goals you set for each part of the organization, each person in the organization, and the whole organization will tell a story that tracks against the cycle of sustainable performance introduced in Chapter 1 and discussed at length in Chapter 7.

Figures 11.1 through 11.4 illustrate the skeletal design of an outcomes management system. Figure 11.1 summarizes the picture for any single business. You see the outcomes that matter most to customers, shareholders, and people of the business; how the outcomes of the most critical initiatives, functions, and processes contribute to overall success; and how the outcomes and goals of small groups and individuals contribute to those initiatives, functions, and processes.

Figure 11.2 extends this single-business view to a multibusiness corporation. In it, you can see how the outcomes of all the various shared service units logically reinforce the outcomes of the businesses to contribute to the outcomes of the corporation as a whole. And each business and shared service unit, in turn, is supported by outcomes of initiatives, functions, processes, small groups, and individuals.

As Figure 11.3 shows, every small group throughout the company should have a performance agenda specifying how the group contributes to outcomes that matter. The top management group of a multibusiness corporation should have a performance

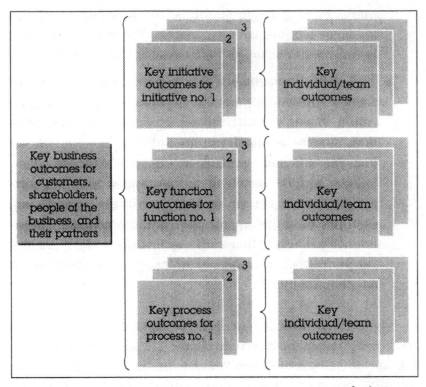

FIGURE 11.1 Business outcomes management system: design.

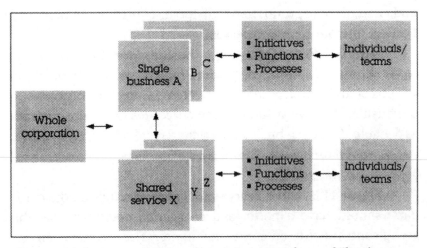

FIGURE 11.2 Outcomes management system for multibusiness corporation.

agenda to drive how its own team and individual outcomes make a difference, and so should small groups that run businesses, initiatives, functions, and processes as well as small groups in middle management and the front lines.

Finally, Figure 11.4 lays out the form of a *personal performance plan* that each person in the company can use to articulate personal aspirations and ensure that their goals and work link to those aspirations. In addition, personal performance plans help people see how their goals fit into the larger scheme of organizational priorities and working arenas.

Figures 11.1 through 11.4 provide the basic elements in an outcomes management system. Figures 11.5 through 11.8 supply

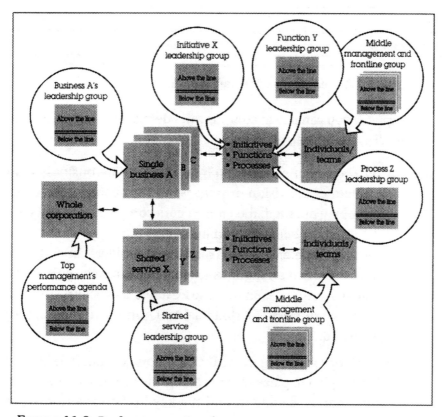

FIGURE 11.3 Performance agendas.

My current aspirations:

Opportunities: _____

_____

_____

Skills: _____

_____

_____

The goals to which I contribute:

Outcomes	Challenge/working arena	Disciplines being used	Link to my personal aspirations
____	_____	_____	_____
____	_____	_____	_____
____	_____	_____	_____
____	_____	_____	_____

FIGURE 11.4 Personal performance plan.

templates you can use to complete the details for each part of the overall system. They include:

- *Business plan summary* (Figure 11.5):   The business plan articulates the vision or purpose of the business, the strategy being pursued, the chosen core competencies and core values of the business, and the overall outcomes that matter most to people, customers, and shareholders. In addition, the business plan requires leaders to tell a story of sustainable performance. Finally, the business plan should include the basic summary of financial and nonfinancial outcomes expected.

- *Initiative plan* (Figure 11.6):   Each major initiative should have a plan in place that describes the purpose of the initiative, who is leading it, and the key initiative performance outcomes that matter to people, customers, and sharehold-

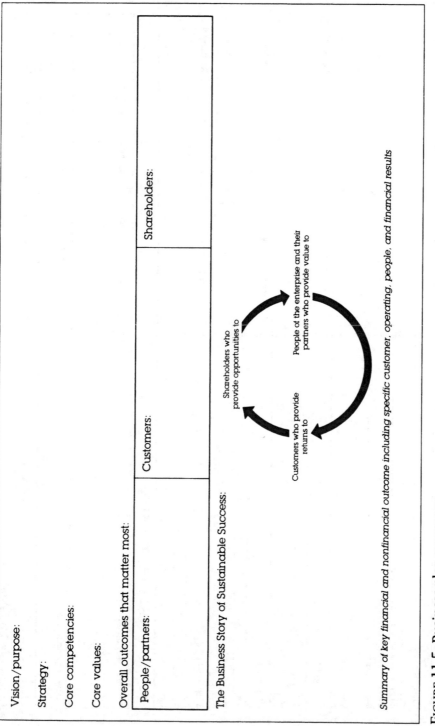

Vision/purpose:

Strategy:

Core competencies:

Core values:

Overall outcomes that matter most:

| People/partners: | Customers: | Shareholders: |

The Business Story of Sustainable Success:

Shareholders who provide opportunities to

People of the enterprise and their partners who provide value to

Customers who provide returns to

Summary of key financial and nonfinancial outcome including specific customer, operating, people, and financial results

FIGURE 11.5 Business plan summary.

Initiative name: _____
Purpose: _____
Initiative leader/leadership group: _____
Overall initiative outcomes: _____
People/partners: _____   Customers: _____   Shareholders: _____

Key priorities

Priority 1: _____   Outcomes/dates _____   Responsibility
Subpriority
1.1 _____
1.2 _____
Etc.

Priority 2: _____   Outcomes/dates _____   Responsibility
Subpriority
2.1 _____
2.2 _____
Etc.

Priority 3: _____   Outcomes/dates _____   Responsibility
Subpriority
3.1 _____
3.2 _____
Etc.

Initiative leadership group's performance agenda			
Priorities we are resourcing	Outcomes	Team/working group discipline?	Responsibilities (names)
Other important challenges we face	Illustrative outcomes that would indicate success		

FIGURE 11.6 Initiative Plan.

ers. Initiative leaders can use the performance tree framework from Chapter 3 to identify the top priorities in their initiatives. For each priority, they should set forth the key action steps, outcomes, dates, and responsibilities. Finally, each initiative plan should include a copy of the initiative leadership group's own performance agenda.

- *Function plan* (Figure 11.7):   Each function should have a plan describing the purpose of the function, who is leading it, and the key functional performance outcomes that matter to people, customers, and shareholders. Function leaders should use the performance tree framework from Chapter 3 to identify the top priorities in their functions. For each priority, they should set forth the key action steps, outcomes, dates, and responsibilities. Finally, each function plan should include a copy of the function leadership group's own performance agenda.

- *Process plan* (Figure 11.8):   Each major process should have a plan in place that describes the purpose of the process, who is leading it, and the key end-of-process performance outcomes that matter to people, customers, and shareholders. Initiative leaders should use the performance tree framework from Chapter 3 to identify the top priorities for their processes. For each priority, they should set forth the key action steps, outcomes, dates, and responsibilities. Finally, each process plan should include a copy of the process leadership group's own performance agenda.

By combining the templates of Figures 11.5 through 11.8, you can create a complete plan for your business. By analogy, you can use the same templates to develop an overall plan for shared service units. If you work in a multibusiness corporation, the set of business plans and shared service plans constitutes the overall plan for your corporation.

Once you have a business plan, you need to use the outcomes specified to conduct regular management reviews of businesses,

Function name: _____
Purpose: _____
Functional leader/leadership group: _____
Overall functional outcomes: _____
People/partners: _____   Customers: _____   Shareholders: _____

Key priorities
Priority 1: _____   Outcomes/dates   Responsibility
Subpriority _____
1.1 _____
1.2 _____
Etc.
Priority 2: _____   Outcomes/dates   Responsibility
Subpriority _____
2.1 _____
2.2 _____
Etc.
Priority 3: _____   Outcomes/dates   Responsibility
Subpriority _____
3.1 _____
3.2 _____
Etc.

Functional leadership group's performance agenda

Priorities we are resourcing	Outcomes	Team/working group discipline?	Responsibilities (names)
Other important challenges we face		Illustrative outcomes that would indicate success	

FIGURE 11.7 Function plan.

Process name: _____
Purpose: _____
Process leader/leadership group: _____
Overall end-of-process outcomes: _____
People/partners: Customers: Shareholders:

Key priorities
Priority 1: _____   Outcomes/dates   Responsibility
Subpriority _____
1.1 _____
1.2 _____
Etc.
Priority 2: _____   Outcomes/dates   Responsibility
Subpriority _____
2.1 _____
2.2 _____
Etc.
Priority 3: _____   Outcomes/dates   Responsibility
Subpriority _____
3.1 _____
3.2 _____
Etc.

Process leadership group's performance agenda

Priorities we are resourcing	Outcomes	Team/working group discipline?	Responsibilities (names)
Other important challenges we face		Illustrative outcomes that would indicate success	

FIGURE 11.8 Process plan.

shared service units, initiatives, functions, processes, and small group performance agendas. In addition, you should regularly review individual progress against personal performance plans. You will need to decide the optimal frequency that makes sense for each of these reviews. Having done that, however, remember to use the reviews for discussion and insight with respect to the following issues and questions:

- How are we progressing against the key outcomes and challenges? Are we on track or not?

- What are the opportunities and risks involved with achieving the outcomes?

- What lessons have we learned regarding how best to achieve our goals?

- What lessons have we learned about which management disciplines make the most sense to use?

- What modifications or additions, if any, should we make to the outcomes we seek to achieve? To the choice of disciplines and/or their application?

- What are the specific next steps needed to achieve our outcomes and plans?

When you combine these outcome-based planning and review steps into a complete outcomes management system, you will transform your organization's performance. You will assure yourselves, your colleagues, your partners, your customers, and your shareholders that you are pursuing the measurable outcomes that matter most to everyone's mutual and sustainable success. You will know how the outcomes you have selected for customers lead to outcomes that matter to shareholders, which, in turn, lead to outcomes that matter to you, your colleagues, and your alliance partners. And you will know how people outcomes, in turn, reinforce the outcomes you seek for customers and shareholders in a story of sustainable performance.

You and all of your colleagues will have clear SMART outcome-based performance goals to achieve. You will know how your goals matter to your customers, your shareholders, and yourselves as well as to the most critical performance challenges facing your organization. You also will know which management disciplines to use for success.

Every small group—whether at the front lines, in the executive suite, or in between—will have a performance agenda setting forth the SMART outcome-based goals the group is resourcing versus those it is not. For each listed goal, the performance agenda will specify the team or working group discipline. The group will use the cycle of performance to set outcomes, pursue success, monitor, adjust, and then move on to new goals (see Chapter 3). When groups do achieve success, they will keep their performance agenda current by moving new goals above the line and assigning resources to them.

Individuals and small groups throughout the company will use the concept of working arenas to map a clear line of sight that connects their goals to larger performance aspirations and outcomes (see Chapter 6). You will understand how individual and team outcomes contribute to the SMART outcome-based goals required for the success of functions, processes, and initiatives. You will know whether vertical/functional performance or horizontal/process performance matters most to the success of your business (see Chapter 9). You will find it clear and easy to map your individual and team goals to function, process, and/or initiative goals and those, in turn, to the SMART outcome-based goals that matter most to the whole business. If you work in a multibusiness organization, you will understand how the SMART outcomes for your business or shared service unit matter to the entire corporation.

You will not suffer from the "spaghetti syndrome." Gone will be the mass confusion and frustration of too many initiatives, too poorly conceived and communicated. Instead, as your organization takes on the multiple challenges required for success in today's world, you will understand how each challenge fits into a larger picture that makes sense. You will connect initiatives, programs, and strategies that primarily benefit customers to those that primarily benefit shareholders to those that primarily benefit you and the other people of your enterprise (see Chapter 7). You will see how goals that you can complete over shorter time frames contribute to goals that will take longer to achieve (see Chapter 7). And you will be able to articulately and confidently explain how nonfinancial and financial goals relate to one another.

When success requires change, you will know when to use the decision-driven discipline and when to use the behavior-driven discipline (see Chapter 10). If you can achieve success through decisions alone, you will make those decisions, communicate them, set SMART outcome-based goals, and get on with success. If, in contrast, you and others must learn new skills, behaviors, and working relationships to achieve success, then you will keep performance results the primary objective of change instead of falling into the trap of change for the sake of change. You will focus entirely on outcomes to sustain the will and the courage to see yourselves through the period of change itself. If you are a leader of behavior-driven change, you will ground your authority in the personal risks you take and the performance commitments you make.

You will manage your organization for performance. And you will manage yourself for performance. You will use SMART outcomes that matter to customers and shareholders to develop the skills, behaviors, and working relationships that matter most to your career, your rewards, your recognition, and your continued participation in your organization. Everyone will have a personal performance plan, laying out how the goals you are pursuing matter to your customers, to your shareholders, and to your own aspirations. When people in your organization reward, recognize, and advise you, they will use your achievements and your opportunities as the basis for working with you to create your own best future. Whether working on outcomes that matter to you, to your customers, or to your shareholders, you and your colleagues will practice those values and behaviors that inevitably sustain high performance. Your organization will be the best place to work. Your organization will be preferred by your customers. Your organization will generate unparalleled returns for shareholders. And your shareholders will enthusiastically support you and your colleagues as you identify and pursue endless opportunities to further benefit your customers, your shareholders, and yourselves.

Appendix

A Field Guide to Making
Success Measurable

As you read and use the tools, techniques, and frameworks in the book, you will discover that they provide a complete, multifaceted approach to setting and achieving performance goals. There are five main themes throughout the book: outcome-based goals, performance challenges, working arenas, balanced attention to constituencies or stakeholders, and management disciplines. Viewed as a whole, *Make Success Measurable!* asks you to answer a handful of central questions about goal setting and achievement:

- Are we setting outcome-based goals that are relevant to the performance challenges we face (instead of activity-based goals)?
- Have we identified the working arenas that are relevant to the performance challenges we face?
- Are the goals we set for the relevant working arenas coordinated and aligned?
- Are the goals we set for all of our performance challenges responsive to the needs of our constituencies (are they "balanced") and are they integrated and linked with one another?
- Do we know which management disciplines to use to best achieve the goals we have set?

The book provides a variety of tools, techniques, frameworks, illustrations, and exercises to help with the challenges and problems associated with each of these broad questions. This field guide, in turn, can help you quickly find the Mindbook and Workbook sections most relevant to the issues you face and the difficulties you seek to overcome. To use the field guide, first identify which of the five broad questions seems most relevant to you. Then find that section of the field guide and identify the more specific question(s) you want help with. For each of these subsidiary and more specific questions, the field guide will point you to the most applicable (1) tools, techniques, and frameworks; (2) figures and illustrations; and (3) exercises.

Section 1: Are we setting outcome-based goals that are relevant to the performance challenges we face?

Question/Issue	Tools, Techniques, Frameworks	Figures and Illustrations	Exercises to Use
Do we even have goals?	Chap 1: Outcomes versus activities; difficulties in articulating outcomes		Exer. 1.1: Mirror, Mirror
Are our goals written down?	Chap 1: Outcomes versus activities; difficulties in articulating outcomes		Exer. 1.1: Mirror, Mirror
Do we have outcome-based goals or activity-based goals?	Chap 1: Outcomes versus activities; difficulties in articulating outcomes	Fig. 1.1: Are your goals activity-based or outcome-based? Fig. 1.4: Reinforcing performance outcomes. Fig. 1.5: The Five Hows. Fig. 1.6: Inputs-impacts-outputs.	Exer. 1.1: Mirror, Mirror Exer. 1.2: How would You Know Success? Exer. 1.3: The Five Hows Exer. 1.4: Stakeholder/ Constituency Analysis Exer. 1.7: Inputs-Impacts-Outputs
Do we have SMART outcome-based goals?	Chap 1: Outcomes versus activities Chap 2: Four yardsticks Chap 3: SMART criteria Chap 3: Performance trees	Fig. 3.1: SMART cycle of performance. Fig. 3.2: Performance tree.	Exer. 3.1: Dialing In Exer. 3.2: Get SMART! Exer. 3.3: Schaffer Funnel Exer. 2.3: Choose Your Yardsticks Exer. 3.5: Performance Trees
Do our goals use good goal grammar?			Exer. 3.4: Good Goal Grammar Exer. 1.4:Stakeholder/ Constituency Analysis Exer. 3.1: Dialing In
Have we picked metrics relevant to the challenge we face?	Chap 2: Four yardsticks; obstacles in choosing metrics that fit Chap 4: New goals for new challenges/hybrid goals	Fig. 1.4: Reinforcing performance outcomes. Fig. 1.6: Inputs-impacts-outputs. Fig. 2.4: Speed/time choices. Fig. 4.2: "Both/and" goals. Fig. 5.3: Indirect arenas/ hybrid goals.	Exer. 2.1: Losing Weight or Feeling Better? Exer. 2.2: Brainstorming and Sequencing Exer. 2.3: Choose Your Yardsticks Exer. 1.2: How Would You Know Success? Exer. 4.1: So What's New? Exer. 4.2: Hybrids
Are we using new metrics for new challenges?			
Are we using nonfinancial metrics for nonfinancial challenges?			

Question/Issue	Tools, Techniques, Frameworks	Figures and Illustrations	Exercises to Use
Will our plans, activities, and efforts lead to outcomes that matter?	Chap 2: Four yardsticks Chap 3: SMART criteria Chap 8: Performance agendas Chap 11: Outcomes management system	Fig. 1.6: Inputs-impacts-outputs. Fig. 8.2: Performance agenda for small group. Fig. 11.3: Performance agendas. Fig. 11.6: Initiative plan. Fig. 11.7: Function plan. Fig. 11.8: Process plan.	Exer. 1.4: Stakeholder/Constituency Analysis Exer. 1.6: Scratching the Activity Itch Exer. 1.7: Inputs-Impacts-Outputs Exer. 2.2: Brainstorming and Sequencing Exer. 2.3: Choose Your Yardsticks
Are we setting new SMART outcome-based goals upon completing earlier ones?	Chap. 3: SMART cycle of performance Chap. 8: Performance agendas	Fig. 3.1: SMART cycle of performance. Fig. 8.2: Performance agenda for small group.	Exer. 3.2: Get SMART
Do we have broad aspirations instead of specific goals? Are we converting broad aspirations into specific goals?	Chap 3: Performance trees; pattern and particulars	Fig. 3.2 Performance tree. Fig. 3.3: MFD's performance tree: phase one/objectives. Fig. 3.4 MFD's performance tree: phase two/SMART outcomes.	Exer. 3.1: Dialing In Exer. 3.5: Performance Trees -
Do our goals have *stretch* in them? Do our goals have "both/and" creative tension? Do our goals have personal tension?	Chap 3: SMART criteria Chap 4: Creative, both/and tension; hybrid goals Chap. 4: Personal tension	Fig. 4.1: Hybrid goals. Fig. 4.2: "Both/and" goals. Fig. 5.3: Indirect arenas/hybrid goals.	Exer. 3.2: Get SMART Exer. 4.1: So What's New? Exer. 4.2: Hybrids Exer. 4.3: Tightrope Walker Exer. 4.4: Better Goal Grammar Exer. 4.5: Throw a Performance Party Exer. 4.6: Work-Out

Question/Issue	Tools, Techniques, Frameworks	Figures and Illustrations	Exercises to Use
Do our outcome-based goals matter to our customers? Our share-holders? Our partners? Ourselves?	Chap 1: Balanced scorecards and cycle of sustainable performance Chap 7: Cycle of sustainable performance; understanding lead/lag and cause and effect	Fig. 1.2: Stakeholders (constituencies) who matter. . . . Fig. 1.3: The cycle of sustainable performance. Fig. 7.3: Cause and effect. Fig. 7.4: The primary thrust and concern of different performance challenges. Figs. 7.5–7.8: Cycles of sustainable performance.	Exer. 1.4: Stakeholder/ Constituency Analysis Exer. 3.1: Dialing In Exer. 4.1: So What's New? Exer. 7.1: Cause and Effect Exer. 7.2: Creating Rein-forcing SMART Outcomes Exer. 7.3: Tell a Performance Story

Section 2: Have we identified the working arenas that are relevant to the performance challenges we face?

Question/Issue	Tools, Techniques, Frameworks	Figures and Illustrations	Exercises to Use
What is a working arena and how does it relate to my job?	Chap. 5: Beyond jobs/ working arenas	Fig. 5.1: Where does performance happen? Fig. 6.5: The working arenas of XYZ Company.	Exer. 5.1: Identifying Your Working Arenas Exer. 5.3: Direct versus Indirect Working Arenas
Are we trying to force-fit all goals into the formal "boxes" of the organiza-tion, such as jobs, depart-ments, and functions?	Chap. 5: Beyond jobs/ working arenas	Fig. 5.1: Where does performance happen? Fig. 6.1: The pyramid model. . . . Fig. 6.5: The working arenas of XYZ Company.	Exer. 5.1: Identifying Your Working Arenas Exer. 5.3: Direct versus Indirect Working Arenas
Have we identified those working arenas, both formal and informal, where the work needed for success will happen?	Chap. 5: Beyond jobs/ working arenas Chap. 5: Fitting goals to working arenas (six questions) Chap. 6: Arena mapping	Fig. 5.1: Where does performance happen? Fig. 6.5: Arena mapping in a single business. Figs. 6.6–6.8: Arena mapping.	Exer. 5.1: Identifying Your Working Arenas Exer. 5.3: Direct versus Indirect Working Arenas Exer. 6.2: Arena Mapping
What are the working arenas that matter most to the success of our performance challenge?	Chap. 5: Beyond jobs/ working arenas Chap. 5: Fitting goals to working arenas (six questions) Chap. 6: Arena mapping	Fig. 5.1: Where does performance happen? Fig. 6.5: Arena mapping in a single business. Figs. 6.6–6.8: Arena mapping.	Exer. 5.1: Identifying Your Working Arenas Exer. 5.3: Direct versus Indirect Working Arenas Exer. 6.2: Arena Mapping

Question/Issue	Tools, Techniques, Frameworks	Figures and Illustrations	Exercises to Use
Have we mapped all the working arenas relevant to the specific performance challenge at hand?	Chap. 5: Beyond jobs/working arenas Chap. 5: Fitting goals to working arenas (six questions) Chap. 6: Arena mapping	Fig. 5.1: Where does performance happen? Fig. 6.5: Arena mapping in a single business. Figs. 6.6–6.8: Arena mapping.	Exer. 5.1: Identifying Your Working Arenas Exer. 5.3: Direct versus Indirect Working Arenas Exer. 6.2: Arena Mapping
What are the working arenas that I or we make a personal contribution to?	Chap. 5: Beyond jobs/working arenas Chap. 5: Fitting goals to working arenas (six questions) Chap. 6: Arena mapping	Fig. 5.1: Where does performance happen? Fig. 6.5: Arena mapping in a single business. Figs. 6.6–6.8: Arena mapping.	Exer. 5.1: Identifying Your Working Arenas Exer. 5.3: Direct versus Indirect Working Arenas Exer. 6.2: Arena Mapping
What are the "smallest" working arenas to which I or we contribute? That is, working arenas composed of a single individual or a single team.	Chap. 5: Beyond jobs/working arenas Chap. 5: Fitting goals to working arenas (six questions) Chap. 6: Arena mapping	Fig. 5.1: Where does performance happen? Fig. 6.5: Arena mapping in a single business. Figs. 6.6–6.8: Arena mapping.	Exer. 5.1: Identifying Your Working Arenas Exer. 5.3: Direct versus Indirect Working Arenas Exer. 6.2: Arena Mapping
What are the larger working arenas to which the results of my/our smaller working arenas contribute?	Chap. 5: Beyond jobs/working arenas Chap. 5: Fitting goals to working arenas (six questions) Chap. 6: Arena mapping	Fig. 5.1: Where does performance happen? Fig. 6.5: Arena mapping in a single business. Figs. 6.6–6.8: Arena mapping.	Exer. 5.1: Identifying Your Working Arenas Exer. 5.3: Direct versus Indirect Working Arenas Exer. 6.2: Arena Mapping
Do the results of my/our working arena make direct or indirect contributions to the performance challenges at hand?	Chap. 5: Problem of indirect working arenas/internal customers Chap. 4: New goals for new challenges/hybrid goals	Fig. 5.3: Indirect arenas/hybrid goals.	Exer. 5.3: Direct versus Indirect Working Arenas

Section 3: Are the goals we set for the relevant working arenas coordinated and aligned?

Question/Issue	Tools, Techniques, Frameworks	Figures and Illustrations	Exercises to Use
Have we mapped all the working arenas relevant to the performance challenge at hand?	Chap. 5: Beyond jobs/ working arenas Chap. 5: Fitting goals to working arenas (six questions) Chap. 6: Arena mapping	Fig. 5.1: Where does performance happen? Fig. 6.5: Arena mapping in a single business. Figs. 6.6–6.8 Arena mapping.	Exer. 5.1: Identifying Your Working Arenas Exer. 5.3: Direct versus Indirect Working Arenas Exer. 6.2: Arena Mapping
Have we set SMART outcome-based goals for *our own working arenas?*	Chap. 5: Fitting goals to working arenas Chap. 1: Outcomes versus activities Chap. 3: SMART criteria Chap. 2: Four yardsticks Chap. 3: Performance trees	Fig. 5.1: Where does performance happen? Fig. 3.1: The SMART cycle of performance. Fig. 3.2: Performance trees.	Exer. 5.1: Identifying Your Working Arenas Exer. 5.2: Match Metrics to Arenas Exer. 5.4: SMART Outcome-Based Goals That Fit Exer. 3.1: Dialing In Exer. 3.2: Get SMART! Exer. 3.3: Schaffer Funnel Exer. 2.3: Choose Your Yardsticks Exer. 3.5: Performance Trees
Do we make indirect contributions to performance? Have we set SMART hybrid goals for our working arenas?	Chap. 5: Indirect working arenas Chap. 4: Hybrid goals	Fig. 5.3: Indirect arenas/ hybrid goals. Fig. 4.1: Hybrid goals.	Exer. 5.3: Direct versus Indirect Working Arenas Exer. 4.2: Hybrids
Do the goals we have set fit our working arenas?	Chap. 5: Fitting goals to working arenas (six questions)	Fig. 5.2: Becoming the best brand.	Exer. 5.1: Identifying Your Working Arenas Exer. 5.2: Match Metrics to Arenas Exer. 5.4: SMART Outcome-Based Goals That Fit
Have we picked metrics that fit our working arena and the performance challenge at hand?	Chap. 5: Fitting goals to working arenas (six questions) Chap. 2: Four yardsticks	Exer. 5.1: Where does performance happen? Exer. 7.4: The primary thrust and concern of different performance challenges.	Exer. 5.2: Match Metrics to Arenas Exer. 2.1: Losing Weight or Feeling Better? Exer. 2.2: Brainstorming and Sequencing Exer. 2.3: Choose Your Yardsticks

Question/Issue	Tools, Techniques, Frameworks	Figures and Illustrations	Exercises to Use
With respect to the performance challenge at hand, do the goals we have set for our working arenas make logical sense when compared to the goals others have set?	Chap. 6: Arena mapping Chap. 6: Qualitative and quantitative alignment	Fig. 6.5: Arena mapping in a single business. Fig. 6.7: Arena mapping in multibusiness corporations. Figs. 6.8–6.9: Arena mapping. Fig. 6.3: The limits of arithmetic. Fig. 6.4: Quantitative and qualitative logical alignment.	Exer. 6.2: Arena Mapping Exer. 6.3: Arena Mapping, Metrics, and Alignment Exer. 6.4: Arena Mapping and SMART Outcomes Exer. 6.1: Finding the Limits of Arithmetic Alignment
With respect to the performance challenge at hand, do our metrics and goals literally add up with the metrics and goals used by others? Do we have *quantitative* alignment?	Chap. 6: Apply qualitative and quantitative logic Chap. 6: Arena mapping	Fig. 6.4: Quantitative and qualitative logical alignment. Fig. 6.3: The limits of arithmetic.	Exer. 6.1: Finding the Limits of Arithmetic Alignment Exer. 6.2: Arena Mapping Exer. 6.3: Arena Mapping, Metrics, and Alignment Exer. 6.4: Arena Mapping and SMART Outcomes
With respect to the performance challenge at hand, do our metrics and goals logically reinforce the metrics and goals set by others? Do we have *qualitative* alignment?	Chap. 6: Apply qualitative and quantitative logic Chap. 6: Arena mapping	Fig. 6.4: Quantitative and qualitative logical alignment. Fig. 6.3: The limits of arithmetic.	Exer. 6.1: Finding the Limits of Arithmetic Alignment Exer. 6.2: Arena Mapping Exer. 6.3: Arena Mapping, Metrics, and Alignment Exer. 6.4: Arena Mapping and SMART Outcomes
With respect to the performance challenge at hand, do the SMART outcome-based goals for our working arenas contribute to the aspirations of the whole organization?	Chap. 6: Arena mapping Chap. 6: Qualitative and quantitative alignment Chap. 7: Cycle of sustainable performance	Fig. 6.5: Arena mapping in a single business. Fig. 6.7: Arena Mapping in multibusiness corps. Figs. 6.8–6.9: Arena mapping. Fig. 6.4: Quantitative and qualitative logical alignment. Fig. 7.4: The primary thrust and concern of different performance challenges.	Exer. 6.2: Arena Mapping Exer. 6.3: Arena Mapping, Metrics, and Alignment Exer. 6.4: Arena Mapping and SMART Outcomes Exer. 7.1: Cause and Effect Exer. 7.3: Tell a Performance Story

Section 4: Are the goals we set for all of our performance challenges responsive to the needs of our constituencies (are they "balanced") and are they integrated and linked with one another?

Question/Issue	Tools, Techniques, Frameworks	Figures and Illustrations	Exercises to Use
With respect to *any single performance challenge,* do we understand how our SMART outcome-based goals matter to customers, shareholders, ourselves, and our partners?	Chap. 1: Cycle of sustainable performance Chap. 7: Cycle of sustainable performance	Fig. 1.2: Shareholders (constituencies) who matter. . . . Fig. 1.3: The cycle of sustainable performance. Figs. 7.5–7.8 Cycles of sustainable performance. Fig. 7.4: The primary thrust and concern of different performance challenges.	Exer. 1.4: Stakeholder/ Constituency Analysis Exer. 7.1: Cause and Effect Exer. 7.2: Creating Reinforcing SMART Outcomes Exer. 7.3: Tell a Performance Story Exer. 7.5: Cascading the Logic of Sustainable Performance
Do we understand the cause-and-effect relationship among the *many different performance challenges* our organization is tackling? Do we understand how these many different challenges fit together to tell a performance story?	Chap. 7: Cause-and-effect relationships of multiple performance challenges Chap. 7: Cycle of sustainable performance/ telling a performance story	Exer. 7.1: Lead/lag and cause and effect. Exer. 7.3: Cause and effect. Fig. 7.4: The primary thrust and concern of different performance challenges. Fig. 1.2: Stakeholders (constituencies) who matter. . . . Fig. 1.3: The cycle of sustainable performance. Figs. 7.5–7.8: Cycles of sustainable performance.	Exer. 7.1: Cause and Effect Exer. 7.2: Creating Reinforcing SMART Outcomes Exer. 1.4: Stakeholder/ Constituency Analysis Exer. 7.3: Tell a Performance Story
With respect to the many different performance challenges our organization faces, do we understand which outcomes happen simultaneously and which ones happen sequentially?	Chap. 7: Simultaneous versus sequential outcomes/time-to-completion analysis	Exer. 7.1: Lead/lag and cause and effect. Exer. 7.3: Cause and effect. Exer. 7.9: USProducts: six challenges.	Exer. 7.4: Arena Mapping and Time to Completion

Question/Issue	Tools, Techniques, Frameworks	Figures and Illustrations	Exercises to Use
Are we able to connect our financial goals with our nonfinancial goals? Do we understand how the achievement of our nonfinancial goals leads to the achievement of our financial goals, and vice versa? Can we tell a performance story for our whole organization? Can we tell a performance story for each of our working arenas?	Chap. 7: Integrate financial and non-financial goals Chap. 7: Cause and effect Chap. 7: Cycle of sustainable performance Chap. 7: Cycle of sustainable performance	Exer. 7.1: Lead/lag and cause and effect. Exer. 7.3: Cause and effect. Fig. 7.4: The primary thrust and concern of different performance challenges. Fig. 1.2: Stakeholders who matter. . . . Fig. 1.3: The cycle of sustainable performance. Figs. 7.5–7.8: Cycles of sustainable performance.	Exer. 7.1: Cause and Effect Exer. 7.2: Creating Reinforcing SMART Outcomes Exer. 1.4: Stakeholder/Constituency Analysis Exer. 7.3: Tell a Performance Story Exer. 7.5: Cascading the Logic of Sustainable Performance

Section 5: Do we know which management disciplines to use to best achieve the goals we have set?

Question/Issue	Tools, Techniques, Frameworks	Figures and Illustrations	Exercises to Use
Do we even have SMART outcome-based goals so that we can use them to choose the appropriate management discipline?	Chap. 1: Outcomes versus activities Chap. 3: SMART criteria Chap. 2: Four yardsticks Chap. 3: Performance trees	Fig. 3.1: The SMART cycle of performance. Fig. 3.2: Performance trees.	Exer. 1.1: Mirror, Mirror Exer. 3.1: Dialing In Exer. 3.2: Get SMART! Exer. 3.3: Schaffer Funnel Exer. 2.3: Choose Your Yardsticks Exer. 3.5: Performance Trees
If the goals we have set are to be achieved by a single small group, for which of these goals should we use the team discipline and for which goals should we use the working group discipline?	Chap. 8: Working group versus team disciplines Chap. 8: Use performance agendas to help make discipline choice in small groups Chap. 5: Working arenas Chap. 6: Arena mapping	Fig. 8.2: Performance agenda for small group. Fig. 8.1: How well are you applying the team discipline?	Exer. 8.1: Choose Your Discipline Exer. 8.2: Develop Common or Mutual Understanding Exer. 8.3: Evaluate Team Progress Exer. 8.4: Put Together a Performance Agenda Exer. 8.5: Use Your Performance Agenda to Conduct an Operating Review of Your Small Group's Performance

Question/Issue	Tools, Techniques, Frameworks	Figures and Illustrations	Exercises to Use
If the goals we have set are to be achieved by multiple individuals and multiple small groups throughout our organization, should we use the vertical/functional discipline or the horizontal/process discipline?	Chap. 9: Vertical/functional versus horizontal/process disciplines for organization-wide performance Chap. 6: Arena Mapping	Fig. 9.1: Working Arenas for a single business. Figs. 6.6 and 6.7: Arena mapping.	Exer. 9.1: Choose Your Discipline Exer. 9.2: Profile Your Effectiveness at using the Vertical/Functional Discipline to Deliver Performance Exer. 9.4: Profile Your Effectiveness at using the Horizontal/Process Discipline to Deliver End-of-Process Performance Exer. 6.2: Arena Mapping Exer. 6.4: Arena Mapping and SMART Outcomes
If our goals require change, should we use the decision-driven discipline or the behavior-driven discipline?	Chap. 10: Decision-driven versus behavior-driven disciplines Chap. 10: Four questions to make choice Chap. 4: Importance of putting hearts/minds into goals.	Fig. 10.1: Do you face decision-driven or behavior-driven change? Fig. 10.2: Wheel of personal change. Fig. 10.3: Paths to decision-driven and behavior-driven change.	Exer. 10.1: Do You Face Decision-Driven or Behavior-Driven Change? Exer. 10.2: Can You Make the Change Decision-Driven? Exer. 10.3: Profile the Effectiveness of Your Decision-Driven Change Effort Exer. 10.4: Specify the "From/To's" of Behavior-Driven Change Strategy. Exer. 10.5: Develop a Behavior-Driven Change Strategy

INDEX

Index

Lightning Source UK Ltd.
Milton Keynes UK
UKOW04n1914061014

239699UK00001B/5/P